Hello Coach!

HELLO COACH!

Victoria Mills

First published 2023

Copyright © Victoria Mills 2023

All rights reserved. No part of this publication may be reproduced, stored in a retrieval system or transmitted in any form by any means, electronic, mechanical, photocopying, recording or otherwise, without the prior written permission of the publisher and copyright holder. Author name asserts the moral right to be identified as the author of this work.

Disclaimer

The contents of this book are general only. They do not represent specific advice or professional advice. You should not rely on the contents of this book in any way. If you need advice, obtain professional advice. To the maximum extent permitted by law, the author and publisher disclaim all responsibility and liability to any person or organisation arising directly or indirectly from any person taking or not taking action based on the information in this book.

Cover design by Sarah Hill

Typesetting by BookPOD

ISBN: 978-0-6456993-0-2 (paperback)
eISBN: 978-0-6456993-1-9 (e-book)

A catalogue record for this book is available from the National Library of Australia

DEDICATION

This book is dedicated to my son, Liam, and my mother, Noelene—my true inspiration and heroes.

I believe if this book has found you, it's happened for a reason. There are no coincidences in our lives and I'm dedicating all of the positivity and encouragement herein to you.

With special love also and deep appreciation to the extraordinary clients I have had the privilege and honor to work alongside, watching your own hero's journey unfold, may you continue to expand your wings and follow the truth of your heart—always.

Victoria x

Sydney, Australia 2023

Contents

Foreword ix
Introduction 1
My story 5
What does a life coach actually do? 13

PART I: THE INGREDIENTS

What you need 21
How this book works 27
Chapter by chapter 31

PART II: CREATING A LIFE YOU WANT

Creating new beginnings 37
What is happiness? 49
Your life's purpose 63
Creating your vision 81
Setting your goal 93
The power of belief 117
Values 129
Affirmations 151
The manifestation Tool 167
Your toolbox 181

PART III: THE DIMENSIONS OF YOUR LIFE

The five dimensions of personal wellness	191
Body	195
Energy	203
Thoughts	213
Checking in	223
Feelings	229
Checking in again	269
Spirit	271
Checking in yet again!	301

PART IV: MAINTAINING BALANCE — 305

The balanced life	307
Living in flow	319

FOREWORD

When I first met Victoria Mills in 2013, I was running Australia's preeminent private art gallery. I was known throughout the country as the son of one of Australia's most distinguished living artists and the brother of the much lauded creator of Dinosaur Designs. I was also fresh from a failed marriage, obese, and confused about my future. I was at an all-time low. I didn't see how I could reconcile my inner turmoil with, what looked to many from the outside, a successful and privileged life.

In my hubris, I believed that I just needed help with my business. I was lacking in time management skills, goal setting, and general organization. A friend recommended that I contact one Victoria Mills, a woman who specialized in focusing on and addressing life issues. I had no real notion of what that actually entailed, but felt that I had nothing to lose at this point.

I was very much challenged by my inability to set boundaries with people, including myself. I believed that I was unworthy of the life that I had—of my heritage, of the love that people showed me. This pain led to me finding ways to validate myself through the eyes of others. I struggled with the specter of my father's recognition and success and his expectations for me. The loss of my mother left me adrift from an emotional foundation that I barely even recognized that I needed. I never felt good enough unless someone else told me so, and then I questioned whether it was real or not, or whether they were just saying so to gain something for themselves. I failed to see that I actually had talents and strengths, all my own, and that I was successful in my own right. It was Victoria who showed me how to recover who I was, and how I could live without fear and recrimination.

Victoria introduced me to her methodology in a tender and reassuring way, telling me with certainty that I had the power within to create the change that I wanted in my life, to become that adult that, as a child, I had dreamed I would become. For most of my adult life, my complex upbringing had made that dream appear to me as a completely unattainable desire. However, through my rigorous and honest work with Victoria, I have been able to create sustainable, positive changes in all parts of my life.

Working with Victoria has been one of the most rewarding experiences of my life. Her intuitiveness, humility, sensitivity, and kindness on every level allowed me to unpack both trauma and success in new and uplifting ways. Her techniques and guidance helped me to identify aspects of myself that I had previously not seen, and face issues that I once found far too confrontational to bear. With her gentle guiding hand, she has provided to me a formula for living that has never let me down and that I continue to use daily. I am now achieving things in my life—healthy relationships with my family, food, friends, and colleagues—that I never thought possible, simply because Victoria has shown me how. I now know how to face my fears with a toolkit that I apply to problems that may arise in my life. Luckily, I have the wisdom now to see obstacles not as problems, just mere hurdles to confront and dismantle in a forthright and positive manner.

Hello Coach!

In this chaotic world, now more than ever, it's evident that we are often unable to visualize and facilitate all the aspects and aspirations that we imagined for ourselves. We are bombarded with external pressures that eventually collide with our own inner conflict and result in a sense of loss—loss of heart, loss of mind, loss of purpose. As Victoria quite generously and simply points out to us, this needn't be so.

The tools, techniques, and systems that Victoria lays out in *Hello Coach!* for us is a game-changer for life. It provides us with an easy-to-follow road map for reintroducing ourselves to our hearts and minds, and in turn to the hearts and minds of our loved ones. It is a way forward with life that makes sense and offers compassion and comfort.

If Victoria Mills is not able to be with you personally, to guide you reassuringly through steps that it takes to make greatness in your life happen, then let her do so with this book. I have worked with Victoria for many years and her approach to life works. I'm healthier and happier than I have ever been, and it's due in large part to the work of Ms. Mills.

I encourage you to find your own pathway to positivity with *Hello Coach!*

Tim Olsen
Sydney, 2023

INTRODUCTION

This book is primarily about finding your deep knowing. It is a step-by-step guide to reclaiming lost lives and repairing broken hearts beyond hope. It is a balm for an overwhelmed life, and a road map for rediscovering the discarded self. Quite simply, it is a manual for reigniting your inner flame to burn so brightly that it may never be extinguished again.

Our greatest gift as human beings is our ability to live in purpose and derive happiness, hope, and fulfillment from within. And yet for many of us this internal "gift" has become so misshapen due to the circumstances of life that it seems more like a burden than a legacy.

But it needn't be so. I have spent close to thirty years studying and working in the field of personal coaching and development and I have witnessed hundreds, if not thousands, of transformations by people from all walks of life—including myself—and I'm here to tell you that living a life you love is absolutely achievable and within reach. By living a more authentic and truthful life, you positively affect—perhaps even inspire—every single person around you and, by extension, the whole planet. But the sad reality is that most of the people I meet do not love their lives; at best, they kind of like them. I don't want that to be your reality. I want you to reclaim your right to a life you will love. I want you to know and reclaim yourself, to step into a more powerful, enriched place within your own life.

It is my ardent mission to support those who seek purpose-driven transformation founded on the principles of love for ourselves, others, and the planet, to find meaning in our existence and to express kindness to ourselves and our fellow human beings. This kind of living is our birthright. Making do, and existing in a space of having the odd, good day here and there, is not enough and quite frankly we can, and should, expect more.

Living a life you love doesn't require ten years of sequestration in a mountainside monastery, outlandish sums of money, a PhD in astrophysics, or a disposition that can never falter. It just requires a realization that your life isn't working as it should and there is a way forward that is attainable, authentic, and possible.

You absolutely can develop a clear, solid foundation from which to create change. In this book, we will work together to formulate an intentional and structured plan so you can change your job, start a new business, buy a new house, increase your confidence, find a loving relationship, or be a better parent. Whatever your life's purpose is, this book will help you to identify it, and make strides toward achieving the goals that you set for yourself. In short, you will become your own life coach. I do not underestimate the size of the task you have ahead of you because I have traveled this road myself and I understand what has brought you here. Not knowing what to do with your life is no joke—it's painful to be without direction.

Over the years as a coach, dealing with clients who felt they had no direction for their lives, I became aware that the biggest issue for many people who want to create change or improve their lives was not that they lacked motivation or discipline; rather, they simply didn't know what to do in order to create change. That change was completely within their power. They *did* know what they wanted in their lives, but identifying *what* they wanted and *how* to go about getting it was where the confusion lay.

Uncovering that roadblock would come as a great surprise to them—and a great relief. And, having identified the issue, I could then get to work designing programs to tackle the client's particular challenge. Just the act of identifying the client's roadblock usually resulted in people waking up enthusiastically and embracing the action required to create change.

I wanted to gather these discoveries and strategies into a book so when you needed guidance you could find it. Mostly, I want you to know that if you are having trouble going after what you want in life because you can't figure out what that want is and how to get there, *you are not alone*. Your problem is a common one and there is help.

You're going to find yourself in these pages. You will reconnect with forgotten parts of who you are and, almost as soon as you recognize yourself, you'll be learning new techniques that can help you, not just with your current situation, but as lifelong methods for self-improvement and happiness. You can do anything once you know what it is you want to do. And you're about to find out.

When you start reviewing your life, the areas you have avoided start showing up like neon lights in a disco. To be successful in creating change, I'm going to provide you with suggestions, guidelines, tools, and challenges to achieve results. Fundamentally, though, everything you need to know is already within you. My job in this book is to help you discover it and unlock it.

I have seen it happen for my clients; I know it will happen for you. The more you know yourself and your unique qualities, gifts, and strengths, the more aware you become of making better decisions in your life in unlimited, positive ways.

By the end of this book, you will discover what inspires you and who you want to be—and then you'll achieve it. It's going to be exciting, enlightening, sometimes a bit painful but also invigorating. Along the way, you will end up adopting some techniques that will become not just life-altering but lifelong methods for addressing issues and releasing yourself from their grip.

This book is not a one-and-done exercise. It's a reference tool that you can return to at any point in your life if you feel that things are not necessarily headed in the direction that you need them to be. We all face challenges at every stage of our existence, but once you know how to identify them and create a set of tasks to overcome them, you will have a skill set that will never fail you. And, to be honest, it's not that hard.

It will take some time and it will take commitment from you, but what other work should you be doing, really? The most important person in the world is *you*. Now you should start living like it.

It takes honesty, courage, and a personal commitment from you if you are to create change. There has to be willingness to change any part of your life, small or big; it doesn't matter which one. But the first question to ask yourself is: "Am I willing to do whatever it takes to create something wonderful and new in my life?" If so, read on!

MY STORY

When I step back and take in the long view of my life, like many of you, I see so much that inspires and surprises me, lifts me up, and also makes me somewhat sad, but mostly I see joy. Hard-earned joy.

Like most people, I've had my share of pain and sorrow, as well as triumph and love, and naturally all the steps that fall in between those two points. When I reflect, I see so many big and small events that have shaped me, people who have guided me and inspired me, and people who have caused me pain, and naturally those that I have caused pain to as well.

However, as I sit here today in 2021, I see a life that I love and am constantly excited about because I have devoted myself to finding a way to create the change that I desperately needed in my early adulthood. Like anything worthwhile, the life that I have created took a long time to build and a lot of hard work to create and sustain, but the sense of happiness and contentment that I have discovered encourages me to keep up the hard work every single day because I believe that I deserve it. That everyone deserves a life of fulfillment, a sense of calm, clarity, and ease.

When I first discovered coaching, I was in my twenties. I'd left behind a childhood ravaged by pain and disillusionment at many turns—my father was a man consumed by his demons, inflicting harm and abuse to those around him and sadly incapable of recognizing or overcoming such toxic behavior. It was being exposed to such harmful behavior that ultimately (many years later) started my quest for answers and solutions to create a different life. My mother was the opposite. Mom was a hard-working perfectionist who loved my brother and me unconditionally and was my rock throughout her entire life. She was not without her own internal pain, but her love of family drove her to keep looking toward the future with hope and quiet courage. She truly was, and remains, an inspiration to me.

After leaving high school, I found myself on the floor of my brother's flat in Sydney's eastern suburbs, keen to start establishing myself in my own right, individually and as a newly minted adult. I'd been doing a bit of modeling to support myself and quickly signed up with Chadwick's, the premiere modeling agency in Australia at the time. I was working steadily with huge names in the international and domestic fashion industry, I was earning money that supported my independence, I was dating, and I truly believed that I could shake the shackles of my unstable past.

It wasn't until I was working in Tokyo that I came to realize that I was desperately unhappy and the world of modeling wasn't really for me. I felt hollow, dehumanized, undervalued, and nothing more than a commodity. My life had been reduced to making clothing look good, no matter how I felt on the inside. It was utterly unsustainable, and I quit. I broke a lucrative contract and flew home to Sydney to try and figure out who I was and how I could begin to feel … something.

The episode in Japan highlighted that I wasn't doing anything that was making my heart happy. What I really craved was some way to be of service to people. I had always wanted to help people, but I lacked the skills, and indeed the inner wisdom, to know how to even begin to approach this mission. As luck would have it, fate stepped in and offered me a chance to take the first tentative steps on what would be my life's journey of helping.

One of Australia's most well-known charities at the time, The Spastic Centre, asked me to participate in the Miss Australia contest, a nationwide fundraising effort that raised money and awareness for Australians suffering with cerebral palsy. Crowned Miss New South Wales in 1992, I spent the year traveling the state, educating others about the condition, and cementing within myself that being of service to others was indeed what I wanted my future to be.

After I finished my term as Miss New South Wales, it was on to bigger things—just as much hard work, but with multinational, recognizable companies like *Vogue*, Murdoch magazines, and Clarins cosmetics. I worked day and night, I had all the trappings of success, and I'd created a persona that I thought brilliantly hid the fact that I was still dealing with internal issues of lack of worth, lack of validation, and genuine disquiet. I was heartsick.

My relationships with men reflected my inner turmoil. I met men who I thought would support my broken inner self, but really I was only attracting those who reflected the pain that I had been suppressing for years. I knew that I wanted to find contentment and happiness within myself and I did all the things that I believed at the time would help me. I attached myself to people as hard-working and goal-oriented as I was and I kept thinking that one day the joy would just turn up on my doorstep if I made enough money, lived in the right house, and projected the right aesthetic. I believed that my internal world just needed to catch up to my external world and then everything would be all right. I could not have been more wrong.

When I finally found myself pregnant and in a failing relationship at twenty-nine, I realized that it was now or never. I really had to stop the merry-go-round that I was on and address the sadness that dwelled inside of me before I brought another life into the world. I was thrilled by the prospect of my baby, but I knew with a sense of clarity and urgency that I had to set my own house in order before I could mother someone.

I'd attempted all sorts of methods of self-healing and knowledge over the years, read books, attended personal development seminars, and looked for ways to exorcise the hurt within but it wasn't until I was introduced to life coaching through a friend that the penny finally dropped for me.

When I met with the woman who would become my coach, she showed me a way forward that would profoundly change my life and provide me with the answers I'd spent years searching for. The way my coach viewed life and our ability to control it with the right techniques and tools connected deeply with my beliefs and desires. What she was offering me—a future that was within my capability to build—made sense to me in a way that no other method had before or since. With her guidance, I was confident enough to leave my marriage with a baby, a suitcase, and a deep yearning to forge a life for myself and my son founded on authenticity, honesty, and safety.

I was mesmerized by the simplicity and effectiveness of coaching and after many months of coaching, I was determined to carve out a professional future for myself. It was truly my soul's calling, and I could not linger any longer. I was ignited by this new avenue of service to others and I set about gaining all the knowledge and the skills that would set me up for a career of showing others how to examine their lives and create meaning and purpose that supports and fulfills their true selves.

It wasn't all smooth sailing, though. While I had found a career path that set my mind and soul alight with joy, I juggled solo parenting and the day-to-day with a niggling feeling that I just didn't quite have all my ducks in a row. There was a shadow lurking over me. Turns out there were in fact two.

At thirty-four, I was diagnosed with a life-threatening illness. This was serious and I needed to address it immediately. Working all the hours that I did and having great success and validation weren't going to mother my child if I didn't stop and get well. I took time away from work and sought the help of the best doctors and health practitioners that I could find—both conventional and alternative. I truly lived my own version of *Eat, Pray, Love*.

I literally did a hard reset on my life, bringing together all the tools and techniques that I had been using for years and that have gone on to become the foundational pillars of my work today: my five dimensions of personal wellness—body, energy, thoughts, feelings, and spirit. What was out of balance, I set about bringing back into peaceful and holistic alignment.

I knew that I ultimately wanted to be a healthy, functioning, and loving adult to my son and myself and that I had to radically address all the facets of my life that were not working. I got better at understanding my health from a nutritional standpoint. I exercised more and found balance with rest. I liberated myself from those around me who were negative and harmful, I prayed, meditated, and changed anything that didn't support my efforts to get well and maintain my health and wellbeing.

In practicing my Five Dimensions of Wellness on myself, I realized that the one impediment that was holding me back, and indeed creating unnecessary chaos in my inner life, was an issue that I'd been suppressing for years: childhood abuse.

As an act of pure love for myself, and with the support of my beloved mother, I found the resolve and strength to confront my abuser, my father. It was at once terrifying, and yet ultimately liberating, and most importantly for me, was the final piece in the puzzle to unbridled freedom from the darkness that had rested within my soul for decades.

It is important for me to qualify my revelation to readers, not simply as a #MeToo disclosure—as valid as they are—but as an example of how recognition of acts of love and forgiveness toward oneself can support vital shifts in the way we can live our lives free of burdens. That being said, all acts of terror, trauma, and abuse are never to be ignored, downplayed, or disbelieved, and help, be that from doctors, therapists, counselors, law enforcement, and others, is important and advised.

Finally, all the pieces of myself—mind, body, and spirit—were aligned as they were meant to be. And while this all sounds rosy, and in some respects it was and continues to be, my life after this point was not without the normal ups and downs that happen in the course of a full and rich existence. I had just found a way to address difficulties, not as calamities but roadblocks to be dismantled and shifted out of my way. My ability to cope and process, stop, assess, and course correct, had been honed and keeps being honed to this very day.

Now, at fifty, I find myself having loved and lost again in the romance department, but I remain hopeful of future commitments that will provide the nourishment that I desire and I look forward to showing to another. I have guided a generous, kind, and smart young man into adulthood and I stand by watching with awe, admiration, and love for everything that he has brought to my life. I have buried parents and friends, mourned and celebrated their passing and continue to practice gratitude for the experiences and love that they have brought to my life.

And finally, back to the work of coaching. It has been, and continues to be, the through line to my life. It has allowed me to heal the shattered parts of myself with care, attention, honesty, and kindness. And it is through my life of coaching and innate desire to be of service that I now find myself able to continue my work with my community, both locally and globally.

After many years of dedication and much work, I launched the internet-based platform, Hello Coach, in 2021, an all-encompassing coaching platform that brings expert coaches—in the fields of love, health, finance, work, personal wellness, etc.—to a central accessible hub that allows for individual one-on-one connection at any time. It truly has been revolutionary, both to me personally and to the many people on both sides of the equation—coaches and clients—that have helped see it through to fruition.

My life's purpose is to provide a mechanism through which people can identify and provide their own hope and purpose. Coaching has allowed me to experience it both personally and professionally.

I am humbled and grateful for the experiences I have had in my life. They have taught me to find courage and strength. They have inspired me to be a better person to myself, my son, my family, and friends and, most importantly now, I have made a difference for others to powerfully create change.

The purpose of this book is to help you reclaim *you* and step into a more powerful, enriched place in your life. Regardless of your circumstances, your life starts with *you*. Take responsibility for yourself and live a life you *love*.

The answer lies within. I invite you to find what inspires the magic that makes you, *you*.

Be brave. Be bold. Be kind. Be love.

WHAT DOES A LIFE COACH ACTUALLY DO?

What a great question! Well, let's start off with another question. Ever wanted to learn to play tennis, cook a great meal, knit, drive a car? These are all skills that you can learn if you hire an expert—a coach—to train you. Much like how an athletic coach guides and supports a talented sportsperson in their athletic pursuits, a life coach guides and supports everyday people in the art of how to look more critically at their life and goals and identify a path toward achieving them with kindness, clarity, honesty, and integrity, propelling the person forward into a life that makes them happier and more fulfilled. Basically, it's your own personal co-pilot helping you navigate the tricky skyways of life so you don't crash and burn; rather, you soar.

Generally speaking, a coach is someone who works with an individual or group in a confidential relationship, either remotely or face-to-face, helping their clients to maximize their strong points and finding ways to organize themselves toward success in every facet of their life experiences.

I found coaching at a time in my life when I was feeling particularly lost, distressed, and confused. A friend suggested I go and see a coach—this was long before life coaching was mainstream or even heard of in Australia. I didn't quite know what I was walking into, but I was so disconnected from myself that I felt I had nothing to lose.

I remember that very first session so clearly. It was just a chat about how this woman worked, what the process entailed, and what I could expect to accomplish from it if I decided to proceed with coaching. For me, it was truly a light-bulb moment. It was like I'd found the ignition switch to turn a better life on, that I could actually change and navigate a new life forward. I had spent years in and out of therapy, searching for answers so as not to feel the way I did, yet with this one meeting, it was like everything up to that point and what I was hearing in that session just coalesced into the future, and it looked bright.

I left that session with a sense of conviction and purpose for what I could and would achieve. My coach had clarified for me that I was more than capable of creating a plan for the rest of my life and achieving it. She had reminded me that I actually had power over my own life, something that had been forgotten by me as I'd made my way to this point—that I truly could take responsibility for my own happiness and create it. And she further empowered me by defining her role as a supportive co-pilot, that she would be there to gently guide me into discovering what it was that I wanted to do with my life, how I wanted to live it, and who I wanted to share it with. My coach literally showed me how to create a map that would change my life forever and build up my strength with tools that would become integral to my life from that day onward. Coaching was, aside from my son, one of the greatest gifts I have ever received and that introduction to it one of the most pivotal moments of my life.

The term "Life Coach" has been thrown around for years and when I first got started in the coaching world, it really was a catch-all for every aspect of life. I'd be called upon to assist business executives in finding a way to climb the next corporate ladder rung, help divorcees reinvent themselves, show people what work/life balance meant, discover ways for others to future proof their lives. Really, it was a bit of everything and it was a fairly new realm for people. It was distinct from therapy or psychoanalysis, and it didn't require expensive equipment or radical medicine. It just required a person wanting to create change to show up and be willing to do the work. It was, and still remains, simple, direct, and effective.

Fast-forward a couple of decades and like anything worthwhile, coaching has evolved and become much more accepted, sophisticated, and widely used. Coaches have morphed into experts specializing in such areas as wellness, career, relationships, parenting, spirituality, sex, leadership, business—you name it and there's pretty much a specialist coach willing to jump into your life to assist you in unearthing the roadblocks and laying the pathway to clarity and fulfillment.

As a pioneer in the field, I still like to cover all the areas of a person's life, but having access to colleagues that have worked deeply in particular arenas is invaluable to me as a coach always striving to improve my own skills.

The last ten years has seen the world develop at an extraordinary rate in terms of technological advancement. We have access to so much more information and content across all manner of devices and ideas. While it's fantastic to be able to shop from our phones and have our every desire met instantaneously, we've all suffered under a staggering weight of disconnection from humankind. Our work/life balance has deteriorated, relationships have become increasingly transactional, and many people have profoundly lost touch with their purpose for living.

As a coach, I've seen this rise in technological disconnection play out in an increasing number of people seeking help to assess and realign their lives. Great for coaches' bank accounts, devastating for the psyche of people. Recent trends in the field have seen coaches focus on "life wellness" or "mental wellness." Clients are finding that their mind and their ability to identify what drives them toward a more fulfilled existence is not as robust as it needs to be, so they turn to coaching to help them figure out a pathway forward. Or put in more simple terms, create a recipe for the healthiest, giant, green smoothie of your life!

If you're hoping to transform your world, a proficient life coach will ask the right questions to help you understand how to break down that transformation process into regular tasks. Each task will be part of what ultimately allows you to self-actualize and attain every goal you set for yourself with your coach supporting you in every aspect of your journey.

Sometimes we have a sense of what we'd like to see happen in our ideal versions of our personal and professional lives but we're not always sure how to go about enacting positive changes. An experienced coach is able to discuss your values with you as a way to identify your true motivations. Once you are aware of the subconscious roadblocks you may have actually put in your own way, you are more equipped to remove them.

Be it at work or in your family relationships or dealings with friends and associates, your coach will be able to help you spot any area that could benefit from a more proactive approach so you can make improvements at a pace to suit you. It's just as important to note that this is not a panacea, nor is life coaching a medical science. At this juncture, it's useful to consider what life coaching is *not*: psychotherapy or psychiatry. With that in mind, this book does not aim to help you explore your psychology in the way that a qualified psychologist or psychotherapist would (and I encourage you to see one of these professionals if you feel it would be of benefit). In this book, I am your remote life coach—I don't get to meet with you in person, but I hope you'll feel that I'm cheering you on. I'm not asking you to do anything more than I ask my clients to do—the difference is that I've documented it all in one book rather than giving you the information and tasks in a series of relevant stages.

Essentially, I'm using all my tested methods of identifying what makes you tick, how those things can help or hinder your personal or professional progress, and creating a road map to move forward, eliminating the things that stand in your way, and elevating your accomplishments toward your goals.

The exercises that you will come across in this book may seem a little foreign to some, easy to others, and downright confrontational to many, but I assure you that they work and you are more than equipped to do this. So, let's get started!

PART I
THE INGREDIENTS

WHAT YOU NEED

I've found over many years that people starting out with coaching come to it with a degree of nervousness, anxiety, and excitement. It's new, after all, and they don't know what to expect, what they're going to need to do or say or collect or reveal. But what they do know, and are determined to achieve, is that they want to make a change. And in order to create the change they're seeking, they need to bring along the following elements: willingness, commitment, desire, and belief.

It's not always going to be easy, but these attitudes are all wholly within themselves and their control.

When I first met with my coaching mentor all those years ago, I brought belief, desire, willingness, and commitment to the table, along with a host of issues that I needed and wanted to overcome. I was certainly a little nervous and a little excited as well, but I want you to know that I've stood where you're standing and felt the emotions that you're feeling, and I have the belief that you can achieve what you're setting out to do right now.

Number 1: Willingness

You need to be *willing* to change. You must want to have a better life. You must want to live a life you'll love and leave behind the life that is currently not serving you. If you don't want to live a life that you love, please don't read any further. I'm serious—come back when you're ready to change. Come back when you're sick and tired of being sick and tired. Then we can work together. But not before.

It's critically important that you understand that working on a new life, a better life, a life that you love, actually means putting in the work to get there. It requires dedication and effort. It's not without a lot of introspection and consideration and care around what you're doing and what you're trying to achieve.

I'll be here with you the whole way and the reward will be more than worth it.

Number 2: Commitment

Next, you're going to need to commit. Yes, commit. That means finding some time in your busy schedule to put aside each day to enable you to make these changes. There's no magic solution to changing your life, and anyone who tells you there is, doesn't really know or understand what it's like to make life-altering changes. Nothing lasting ever happens quickly; nothing good comes without work. You'll need time and you'll need to understand that there's some work involved, and to bring those two key elements together, you need commitment. But you're not on your own; we're doing it together. By asking you to dedicate time to this work, I mean that you should get out your diary or go to your online calendar and actually schedule in some time for you. I will be setting tasks for you to do, and you'll need to make them a priority, because they *are* a priority.

Remember, as I have said: no one is more important than you.

The process you are about to experience may take you a few weeks or it may take you a few years—it all depends on how ready you are for each step. Don't put any pressure on yourself to complete any stage by any given time; however long it takes is the right amount of time for you. All I'm asking for is a commitment to believing that all the time, work, and energy that you are putting into yourself will be worth the effort. Although I will ask you to set certain goals and intentions, you don't need to set a time-based goal.

Number 3: Desire and belief

I believe that desire and hope are two interconnected feelings that are inextricably bound to acceptance or belief. For me personally, faith and belief are the ultimate union, my spiritual best friends who have remained by my side throughout some of the most turbulent storms of my existence. My belief and faith in hope and desire has been strained over the years—like many people's. Life can brutalize you. But they have always been the sanctuary to which I have returned. Battered perhaps, but wiser and stronger, nonetheless.

As humans, we can all become disillusioned with our lives at various times. We can feel lost and so far away from who and what we thought we were, that we desperately question what our purpose in life truly is. This critical point can present as a job that crushes us, a relationship on the brink of collapse, financial calamity, or a great big hole where our self-esteem used to live.

And yet, hope can remain. Hope for something better. A better life, a healthier relationship, more job satisfaction, greater abundance. It is at this moment in our lives, when everything that we know seems to be broken and falling apart, that we register a flicker of hope that fuels our desire for change.

From acknowledging our hopes and desires, we are assisted by belief and faith—belief in ourselves, our abilities, and whatever wisdom that upholds us, to make the changes that will allow us to live bigger, better, more fulfilling lives.

This book offers us a return to hope and provides us with the resources to achieve our desires and realign our faith and belief in the sustenance that we are more than capable of delivering to ourselves. *Hello Coach!* allows us to see the connections between our trust and faith in our own selves, and how that understanding enables us to live up to the hope that we have for something more substantial in our lives.

The one common ingredient in coaching is that it creates the shift in our behaviors that move us from unfulfilled to fulfilled. It is a combination of the desire for a better life, the willingness to believe in a better life, and the commitment to the movement toward a better life that makes coaching so effective.

We are not here in this life to sit on the couch of resignation and stagnate; we owe it to ourselves to fulfill our dreams and live our life in a state of happy purposefulness. As human beings, we deserve to have a life of passion that fills us up mind, body, and soul. We shouldn't settle for just taking up space in this world.

When I first found coaching, I was in an unhappy marriage with a very young baby. I was holding on to the belief that there had to be something more out there, something bigger, something better, but I just didn't know how to get there. I held the desire for change and the belief that not only was it possible but that I could do it, deep inside of me, but I lacked the know-how to move forward.

Those first few coaching sessions allowed me to connect the belief I had in a better life and the commitment and willingness I was prepared to put into the creation of a better life for myself and my baby. I rediscovered the beautiful parts of myself that I wanted to hold on to as I navigated my way through pain, sadness, and just general clutter in my life that was utterly superfluous. I was deeply committed to making my life better, to seeing something better for myself and my son.

Becoming a parent has been, without a doubt, one of the most profound experiences of my life. Many parents say this and the cliché is very true. It changed my heart in ways that I find difficult to this day to describe. Everything in my life that got me to my child—every hardship, every success, every failure, every questionable turn—it was all worth it, but what parenthood gave to me, outside of my beautiful child, was the realization that I had owed it to myself and to him to blaze a trail toward a life that I loved, and to fully commit to living that life. I wanted to show him that there was no need to compromise and live a life of miserable frustration or boredom, that commitment, willingness, belief, and desire were all states of being that could help him build a life based on a system of personal values that inspired a legacy for his children and his family, and created richness within himself and the world around him.

I believe that lives lived this way are for everyone, no matter who you are, where you live, or what you do. Powerful change is possible when the work is done.

HOW THIS BOOK WORKS

I don't know how many times I have said the same thing to myself throughout the process of writing this book: I wish that I'd had this go-to manual when I was going through my own personal journey of change! It's one of the reasons that I decided to do the book in the first place; to have all my theories, philosophies, and techniques in a handy compendium that can be used over and over again.

Essentially, this is a road map for change that centers upon my concept of the Five Dimensions of Personal Wellness: body, energy, thoughts, feelings, and spirit. You can't fix one element without impacting the others, and they are all interconnected and equally important.

When we wish to effect significant change in our lives, most of us are not looking for just one thing to be different, even if it may start out that way. We're looking for a dramatic overhaul, so it makes sense that we, as multidimensional beings (mind, body, and spirit), would want to look deeply and comprehensively at all the aspects of who we are and activate transformation in all those areas. This is a journey that requires us to realign all the parts of who we are so that we can experience wholeness.

It's also really important to understand that change on the level that we're talking about is fundamentally a healing process that needs to take place without guilt or shame. We cannot erase our past, but we can view it from a calm, kind, and clear-eyed perspective that allows us to investigate the events that have shaped us and where we need to make some adjustments. I believe one hundred percent that we are all worthy of living powerful, extraordinary lives.

The book is laid out in such a way that we move through chapters progressively, with tasks and challenges that build on each other. You do not have to move any faster than you want to; nor do you have to move more slowly than you want to. The pace is yours to set. But I strongly recommend that you follow the order of the chapters and perform the tasks as they are laid out to get the most out of your effort and commitment. In all my years as a coach, I have tested this exact process of change over and over again, and it always works.

By using the coaching steps in this book, you will uncover the internal changes first. When you find yourself again and feel happier, healthier, calmer, or whatever it is you are desiring, you will realize that your external world has changed as if by magic; however, it is merely a reflection of the new you that you have created.

It is important to understand that you cannot reach your final stage of change—on the level of spirit—unless you move through the physical, intellectual, emotional, and energetic changes first. It's simply not possible. If it were, I'd definitely tell you. So, no matter how much you want to accelerate this process and skip steps, please don't. Believe in the process and success will follow.

Everyone's time is a precious commodity. I'm here to help and support you. And I know that this process works. I believe that shift happens with time, willingness, and commitment, and I know that you're ready to tackle these things; otherwise, you wouldn't be here. This book is a guide that pulls all the information together and structures the exercises into a method of achieving the life you've been looking for. This book is your best friend, your inspiration, your wisdom, and your guidance.

As we know, best friends tell the truth. I want this book to be able to get you to tell the truth about who you are and how you're limiting your own life. And I also want the book to be a source of nourishment, to help you love who you are.

When I started out on my journey of change, I didn't have a book to help keep me aligned to the course I was charting. I made mistakes and change didn't happen at the rapid pace I wanted it to. I faced challenges that I didn't understand that took me way off course, but I honestly believe that those hurdles slowed me down for a reason. They made me stop and appreciate what I was doing and how I needed to refine my methodology. By bringing together in one place all the tools and techniques that I use with clients on a day-to-day basis, I feel that this book will fast-track you to achieve what you want.

Even today, I refer to the exercises and techniques set out in *Hello Coach!* when I'm feeling confused, overwhelmed, or facing difficulty. Being able to find focus and comfort in the simple how-to's of this book clarify my thinking and ground me so that I can analyze, strategize, and move forward toward a happier and healthier place. And so can you.

Some of the work we'll do may seem a bit esoteric to you, particularly as we move into the realm of spiritual change. It's quite all right to be skeptical—but I also need to emphasize that every person I have worked with has only really embedded positive change into their life by addressing their spirituality. Many of us live in what you could call a spiritual deficit, whether or not we realize it, and it's not until we address that lack that we can truly say that we're happy. On some intrinsic level, I'm sure you know that this is true for you too.

It's important to add at this point that I have no religious agenda to push, nor do I harbor any particular spiritual beliefs that I think you should follow; rather, I am opening up to you the notion that spirituality is present in our lives and it is up to you personally to embrace what that means to you. For some, it's God and Christianity in all its forms, for others it might be mysticism, Hinduism, Buddhism, Islam, Shamanism, Spirit, Source, The Universe. Whatever you believe is where you need to place your spiritual focus. I have left plenty of space for interpretation in this book, meaning that when you reach the part of the text that requires you to consider your own personal spiritual understanding, you do so within the confines of what you believe. I may refer to God, Source, Spirit, or The Universe, but I want you to put your own spin on that and use a term that is meaningful to you.

There is really nothing holding us back at this point, so let's get to work.

CHAPTER BY CHAPTER

In each chapter, I'm going to provide you with examples and directions that will act as a guide to help you complete each task. I'll be standing by as your co-pilot the whole way, on hand to help at any time.

The essence of these chapters is to equip you with deeper insight into who you are and all that you want to be. It will help to create greater hope and the new possibilities that are waiting for us to discover together. My greatest wish as we travel through these pages is that each one ignites a little more light and belief and champions you forward.

To align all the dimensions of who we are—remember the Five Dimensions of Personal Wellness: body, energy, thoughts, feelings, and spirit—we need to bring them together in a way that makes sense in your life and in a routine that works for you. Then, at the end of each chapter, there will be tasks that I will ask you to undertake, such as:

- Daily affirmations
- Quiet space each day for prayer and meditation
- Journaling or the "mind chatter" dump
- Visualization
- Setting and reviewing your goals and intentions.

None of these tasks is beyond the capability of anyone I have met in the course of my work; nor are they beyond you. It doesn't matter if you've never used visualizations before, or meditated, or kept a journal.

You will learn as you go through this book, at the right time and in the right way. No specialized knowledge is required for this book to work. You just have to be you, but it's important that you do these tasks, as they will help you get to know yourself better.

They are meant to be challenging and, sometimes, confronting. Please don't be put off by them, because they are the small steps needed to create lasting change.

Your last job in each chapter will be to complete the review.

As a personal coach, I became a partner in my clients' lives as much as I was a cheerleader. During sessions, we'd re-evaluate their goals and priorities, redefine what success was for them based more on a holistic approach than just material possessions and wealth, and help them discover what they truly wanted and desired. After each session, clients left with an action plan to be completed by the next session.

I noticed how these small weekly changes produced some big results so in each chapter we will evaluate your progress as though we are sitting side-by-side. These review steps become measurable milestones to track your progress and help you achieve your goals. It's really important to not move on to the next chapter without answering your questions, completing your tasks, and undertaking your review.

Okay, so if you try to skip anything, there's just no way the next phase of your change is going to take shape. And, yes, this is going to take a bit of your time, but there really is no rush. You are setting your own pace here.

I hope that by now your confidence about the journey you're embarking upon is high, and your level of excitement is matching it, because you have earned it. You've decided that the time is right to make monumental changes in your life. You've made the first step toward the future. So, with that being said, now is the time for you to be your own coach. I'm cheering you on!

PART II

CREATING A LIFE YOU WANT

CREATING NEW BEGINNINGS

Are you the type of person who is filled with excitement at the thought of something new? Or maybe you're terrified, or just somewhere on that massive continuum. New can be challenging, it can be hard, and it can be confronting. But just as scary as "new beginnings" can be, they can also be wonderful and thrilling and liberating. Regardless of your approach to new beginnings, one of the most frequent impediments to starting something new that I see time and time again in my practice is the question of where to start? This question can be absolutely paralyzing for people, but it needn't be.

Almost everybody that I've ever worked with has faced some degree of dilemma over the questions of where and how to start. This can lead to either giving up before you start because it's too hard, or a total frozen-with-fear anxiety about not being able to even locate a starting point. I believe that starting something new doesn't have to be scary or debilitating. It just has to be.

You may be thinking that you don't know where to start, how to start, or maybe you're wondering why you're actually starting. But trust the decision you have made to undertake this process of change, because that is the start. You've already started!

You have come to the realization that you needed to make a change and that change is a new beginning. You know that you need to do things differently. That knowing is the feeling you have when you're drifting off to sleep at night, or waking up first thing in the morning, simply knowing that you cannot tolerate another day of living a disingenuous life.

Now let's find out which areas of your life you can begin to change.

My own new beginning started when I decided to leave my marriage. I was actually being coached myself and after the third session, I had enough insight and knowledge to know that I would be dishonest with myself if I stayed in the marriage, because there was no love and I didn't want to stay there out of fear.

Once I had made the decision to leave, I had crossed the threshold of uncertainty that often accompanies change and new beginnings. I then made a plan. It was a very well-thought-out and considered strategy of how I was going to do all the things I needed to change my situation. That plan included details on how I would financially support myself for the next twelve months, packing my bags and my son's bags and moving out, and finding a new place to live. I also had a vision that after I finished coaching as a client, I wanted to set up my own practice as a coach. My new beginning and first steps toward happiness were all done in the space of a few months from having undergone some sessions of life coaching. Those sessions had literally given me the guidelines and confidence I needed to start really digging into the detail of how I would bring about the change I was seeking.

I put into practice what I was learning as a client, which was to get really clear about what I actually wanted in my life, what my life entailed in terms of my health, what I wanted for my career, how much money I wanted to make in my new business, what that new business looked like, how I wanted to parent my child, and how I was going to support myself. I had a really clear, strategic plan designed for my new beginning.

But before all of that planning I, like most people that are suffering, had to embrace the real kick-in-the-guts feeling that I was at a turning point in my life. I could no longer carry on in the way that I was. Life was not working. I was not working. I was unhappy and unfulfilled. But I knew, deep within myself, that I had the ability to make this better no matter how terrifying the future looked. I just had to commit to change. That first step into the unknown is always the hardest, but once I had decided to make the change, I then began the work of figuring out how to do it.

And, as you will see when you move through this book, your own new beginning will turn into a vision and a plan for your new life.

Making your list

When I first go into a coaching session with a new client, I like to ask them a set number of questions that will give us a little bit of a framework to understand where they find themselves at this particular moment in time. It enables both parties to get some clarity around the journey they're embarking on and helps me to put the guide rails in place to see the client succeed. The list below contains some of the common reasons people seek out a coach. These are not goals, but rather a window into their current life, right now.

This list might inspire you in other areas of your life that you haven't previously considered as an area for change.

Would you like to:

- Achieve a goal or ambition?
- Reduce the amount of stress in your life?
- Improve your communication skills?
- Clear the clutter that holds you back?
- Change or improve your career?
- Improve health, wellbeing, and fitness?
- Increase self-confidence or your self-esteem?
- Attract a loving relationship and partner into your life?
- Improve the balance between work and home life?
- Change the direction of your life?
- Become more focused on what you want and why you want it and how you can get it?
- Enable yourself to reach your goals, or accomplish your own dreams and ambitions?
- Create greater financial prosperity?
- Pursue a lifelong dream but you don't know where to start?
- Improve your parenting skills?
- Get clarity with an unresolved issue?

Not all of the things listed will resonate with you; however, there will be at least two or three areas that you know you want to change. And if you have made the decision to start this process of change and you have committed the time to it, that is already a new beginning. I usually encourage my clients—and I now encourage you—to honor that new beginning by making a silent pledge to yourself. If you feel challenged over the coming weeks, use this pledge to keep your focus and remind yourself of the reasons you chose to start this process of change.

As soon as the going gets tough, or you find yourself becoming distracted, or you start asking yourself, "Why am I doing this?", always remember that you're doing it because you chose to.

That's all and that's enough. You don't need a better reason. Just put one foot in front of the other and do not stop. Take a break by all means, but do not stop. That's how you stick to your commitment.

It's your decision whether or not you tell anyone else about what you're doing, but I believe that this commitment that you're now making is only for you. It's your promise to yourself to maintain the promise that you have made to yourself.

Task 1: Reflecting and reviewing

Let's begin your personal transformation in a positive way by reflecting on the previous year in your life and reviewing what's worked well.

Often when we start to think about making any change, there can be a part of ourselves that sends a subtle message to our brain and body that somewhere inside the person we define as "me" there is a tiny particle that isn't quite good enough, not whole enough, or the opposite—we are too much!

Our brains and our daily thought patterns can play havoc in our lives when we listen to this voice repeating the same message over and over. A negative mindset can break us down and weaken our beliefs about ourselves and threaten our self-esteem.

The outcome of this exercise is to remind you that there *is* good in your life, and positive reinforcement is crucial in this journey as you start to unravel the layers that make up your life.

As you reflect over the last twelve months, write down the answers to the following questions:

What three qualities have you discovered that you really like about yourself?

1. _____
2. _____
3. _____

What special events and memories have you created with those you love?

1. _____
2. _____
3. _____

Can you describe some aspects of what makes you happy? For example, did you take a holiday or spend time somewhere that made you feel amazing?

1. _____
2. _____
3. _____

List three projects or hobbies that you undertook and are proud of:

1. _____

2. _____

3. _____

Task 2: Reintroducing you to you

Creating a brand-new life starts with you. Lasting change takes time and patience, so don't rush around trying to catch up on stuff you didn't get to do in the past. This kind of manic behavior doesn't create lasting change. In fact, it slows you down and distracts you from focusing on the present and the future. Racing through these processes and not giving due consideration to your thoughts will lead to confusion. So, pause, take a deep breath, and focus.

You were born with qualities that no one else has and at some point in your life, for whatever reason, you have forgotten about these special attributes that make you unique. One way of helping you rediscover these attributes is to acknowledge yourself and appreciate yourself. So, let's take a moment to answer the following questions.

The outcome of this task is for you to reintroduce yourself to the forgotten aspects of who you are.

When you take time to recognize and congratulate yourself for everything you are and everything you do, you will start to see changes happening quickly. As you do this you will find that your mood lifts, your self-confidence grows, and your energy improves.

What do you love about yourself? If you were to describe yourself to someone else, how would you do it in two sentences?

I'm_____

And_____

If you asked a family member, partner, or best friend the top three things that make you special, what would they be?

1. _____
2. _____
3. _____

In what areas of your life do you let yourself shine? Acknowledge yourself right now. Write down five things that you appreciate about yourself:

1. _____
2. _____
3. _____
4. _____
5. _____

Your affirmation for new beginnings

I encourage you to start practicing the magic of affirmations. I'll go into more detail later in the book; however, for right now, all you need to know is that affirmations are short, simple statements that can affect the way you think and feel. And trust me ... they really work! Say the following affirmation on the next page each day as you go about your affairs and write it out each day when you have a quiet moment. In its subtle way, the affirmation will start to shift your thinking in a more positive direction. And to paraphrase Gandhi: thoughts become words, words become actions.

As I mentioned earlier, some of the things I ask you to do may seem a bit esoteric, and this could be one of them. But affirmations are so simple to do that even if you don't believe in them, what do you have to lose? All you have to do is repeat the following statement to yourself whenever you think about it, then write it down in your notebook whenever you have a spare moment. That's it.

"I love and accept myself unconditionally and I am kind to myself during this process of change."

Your daily task

Each morning as you're going through this process of change, take some time out to write in your journal or a notebook any and all negative thoughts that might be getting in the way of your happiness. The thinking behind this exercise is that by dumping out unhelpful and cluttering "mind chatter," you're freeing up space for positive thoughts to flow in. It's also a great way to start out your day with a positive mind frame.

There is no right or wrong way to do this, and you can take as little or as much time as you need, but getting in this habit does fast-track change.

I want to take a moment here to distinguish between "mind chatter" dumping and journaling. Both are exercises that I fully endorse and participate in personally, most days.

As I've explained, "mind chatter" dumping is a way of just getting all the negative thoughts out of your head before you start your day. It puts you in the great position of having space for positive thoughts. No one needs to see what you've written, and it can just be points or notes. It doesn't require a great deal of analysis or particularly well-formed sentences.

Journaling, however, is a little bit more of a process. Journaling lends itself to deeper thought and contemplation because it's a technique that relies upon you thinking more critically. This can be a great forum for you to really explore all the positive thoughts and aspirations that you have in a really detailed way. It can also be a recording of things that have happened throughout the day and simply a place where you jot down important pieces of information that you need to remember.

I have a client that takes a hybrid approach to the "mind chatter" dump and journaling. She tends to work through her issues in the written form and move from the negative space into the positive space working through what's happening in her life. This method works for her because she's refined it over a number of years.

Personally, I spend about five to ten minutes each morning purging negative thoughts from my mind. It can be as simple as being tired by the prospect of cleaning the house to being annoyed that a work project has missed a deadline. Whatever it is, I just jot down a note in a "dumping book" and then move on. After all the years of practicing this technique, I've found that it really sets me up to calmly and positively approach my meditation and prayer practice. I just have such a better attitude going into it when I've cleared my mind of thoughts that I don't need to process.

It's also super helpful with my own practice of journaling. I keep this space pretty sacred and only about the positive because I find that it reinforces my gratitude practice when I do. When I'm solely focused on the positive aspects of things—and it can pretty much be anything these days because I'm committed to finding silver linings as much as possible—I find that my general day-to-day mental wellness and physical health are so much more easily maintained.

The big takeaway right now is that I'd like you to start with the "mind chatter" dump and work your way up to journaling if you wish. Again, there's no right or wrong here, there's just consistency and what works for you.

Your review

At the end of each chapter, and the completion of the assigned tasks and affirmations, I'll ask you to review how you felt about the tasks and their outcomes, what your experiences were once you looked more deeply at your thoughts and desires, and any extra commentary that is worth recording. A review of the tasks and affirmations will cause you to really think about the discoveries that you've made and help to bed down the new thoughts that are beginning to take shape.

You can tackle this review a couple of ways; you may wish to write down the answers to the review questions in your journal or you can just say the answers out loud to yourself. There's no right or wrong way to approach this exercise, it's about what works for you.

1. What were my personal highlights?
2. What challenges did I face and how did I handle them?
3. What new insights into myself did I discover?
4. What is my greatest achievement in this phase?
5. What is my commitment for the next chapter?

Remember

By the end of this book, you will discover what inspires you and who you want to be—and then you'll achieve it.

Your checklist

A. Complete Task 1: Reflecting and reviewing.
B. Complete Task 2: Reintroducing you to you.
C. Write out affirmation and verbalize each day.
D. Your daily task: "mind chatter" dump.
E. Complete review.

WHAT IS HAPPINESS?

Let's kick this chapter off with a doozy—what is happiness to you? Yes, that's right—to you. Not to your husband, boyfriend, girlfriend, mother, best mate, dog, guinea pig, or child. What is happiness to you? Can you define it in words, feelings, thoughts, and experiences? Can you articulate how it smells, feels, tastes, and looks? Have you been happy in the past? Do you allow yourself to be happy in the present, or do you hope that you will find happiness around the corner "when things are different"?

To me, happiness is an overrated, overused, fluffy term that people are attached to, yet don't use with authentic intention or even moderate understanding. Now I don't want you to misinterpret what I'm saying. I like happiness and I strive to achieve it in my daily life, but I want to be very frank with you. I've done a lot of work on understanding what makes me happy and how I can continue to practice happiness on a daily basis. What I want from you is for you to recognize what your happiness is and how it operates in your life. What is it that truly makes your heart sing?

In this chapter, you will work on understanding that you want to create happiness in your life and defining what your own version of happiness actually looks like; figuring out which elements need to come together in order for you to say, "I'm really content and happy."

I can't stress this enough—you already know what defines you, because what defines you and what makes you happy is completely different from what makes anyone else in the world happy.

In my experience, too many people believe that there is a certain way of living and thinking that is conditional upon what other people do, say, or think. They equate happiness with possessions, money, careers, and objects that other people possess. A common refrain that I hear from clients is that "my parents had this and they were happy" or "my friends do this and they are happy." There's no real way of knowing if these people are happy or not because most people go through their lives putting on elaborate displays and facades that deliver the illusion of happiness to the outside world.

You need to be able to stand tall and apart, and work out what you specifically need in your life for you to then be able to say you're happy. Simply saying "I want happiness" and not working on your own personal definition of what happiness is to you will not result in you being happy. We need to discover and define what happiness is to you, so that you can a) work toward it, and b) recognize and rejoice in it when you achieve it.

If you're not happy, it's really important to ask yourself why.

In my many years working as a coach, I have lost count of the hours I have spent philosophizing about what happiness is. How do we find it? Am I really worthy of it? What does it feel like? Am I meant to feel happiness each day? When I have asked clients about what happiness is for them, they have had a hard time trying to tell me and have more easily explained the absence of happiness in their lives. Just about universally, most people tell me that it feels as though something is missing. And furthermore, they are not actually able to articulate or pinpoint exactly what that missing element is.

A lack of happiness is often exacerbated by the elusive thought that happiness is just minutes away. We kid ourselves that happiness is around the corner, never here in the present. "If I could just find a better house, then I would be happier!" we may say, or "If I could find a better job, then I'm sure I would be happier!" or "If the kids were less demanding, then I would have more time to myself and then I would be happy and content!" or "If my husband was less moody then the whole house would be happier!", or my favorite, "If I could just find a great partner, then it would solve all my problems and I would be happy!"

Then the ideal partner, or job, or house comes along and brings its own problems and challenges … so we question our happiness all over again. We have just jumped on the perpetual hamster wheel of the ever-elusive, just-around-the-corner happiness that never quite seems to materialize. It's debilitating and frustrating and it causes us to stop focusing on improvement as we compare ourselves to others who we think are happy, and castigate ourselves for not being able to achieve this state of happiness. It's a vicious cycle that we just don't need to participate in.

My own awakening with understanding what happiness was to me came about with the birth of my son. When I held him in my arms, I truly understood that I needed to be the most effective mother I possibly could be so that I did not project any of my own unhappiness on to him.

I vividly remember bringing my son home from the hospital and the deep wellspring of unconditional love that washed over me. I was watching him sleep in his crib and the love for him was so overwhelming. I had never felt this degree of love for anyone in my life before. It was unadulterated joy and this bliss truly brought me so much happiness. It still brings me happiness when I see him each day, many years past his newborn state.

Along with all this peace, joy, and happiness came the realization that it was my responsibility as his parent to guide him into adulthood to the best of my ability and for me to do that I had to be very solid in my own internal peace, calm, and happiness, which at the time, aside from my son's existence, I was not.

I have learned over the years that we can only gift to others what we gift to ourselves, and with that in mind I set forth to really understand how I could be the best possible example to my son as he grew through his own life. I wanted to make sure that I was diligent about paying attention to who I was and how I could grow into a better version of myself, while developing a deep connection to my son and giving him the same opportunity to be happy and confident about who he is as a human being. Being his mother has been one of the greatest gifts I have ever experienced in my life and from it I have been able to grow, adapt, and find the happiness that I thought would elude me forever.

His birth also coincided with my blossoming love affair with coaching. I had the chance to design a life I loved based on my values. Based on what I wanted and needed to thrive in life rather than have my decisions based on fear.

Life will always give us the chance to start again, to make new decisions. However, we can't move into the new life if we carry around old belief systems and ways of behaving. It's not just our mindsets that may need overhauling; it's our bodies, our hearts, our spirit, and emotions that need a good clean out. Coaching gave this to me. It gave me a map that would help me stay focused and clear on my journey, and a path that so inspired me that I required very little motivation to put in the time and resources to achieve my goals. The happiness that I discovered from the birth of my son and the power of coaching lit a fire in me that continues to burn brightly to this day. That fire I call my beacon of hope.

Many of us have lives that are chaotic and rife with desires and expectations. We collectively tell each other—if not directly then subtly through cultural means—that we must have a perfect life with, say, a lifelong soulmate, perfect kids who make us proud of their achievements, friendships that are deep and meaningful, a rich career, a full social life—and that's just on the surface. We brutalize ourselves with this constant nagging need to achieve, achieve, achieve! And we mistakenly equate happiness with some sort of measurable means of success. Long-lasting change does not happen this way; happiness cannot be found if we seek to find it in external objects and gratifications.

We just keep raising the benchmark, replacing our achievements with the next bigger and better goal, not wanting to stop and truly face the void, or whatever disquiet is within us, that propels us to keep doing, pushing, achieving toward a level of overload and, ultimately, unhappiness. When we spend time seeking happiness from the outside world rather than from looking within, we rarely discover authentic, deep happiness. Instead, our misery and lack of satisfaction continue to grow nourished by our inability to face ourselves and our unhappiness because that would require not only some work, but also some inner reflection that may cause us to shine a light on some pain that we have been purposely ignoring.

We need to take a step away from this turbulence and chaos and stop, breathe, and take some real inventory about how we define happiness.

Your version of happiness

If you feel dissatisfied with your life, or feel as though something is missing, you may want to consider this: it might just be that what's been missing from your life is you.

Whether it's a client or a friend talking about feeling unhappy and unfulfilled at work, or a reader who asks for help in finding her lost self amid the daily madness of work, raising a family, relationship challenges, financial stress, or health issues, I've found that many of us are struggling to find more meaning and a sense of purpose in our lives. We are struggling to find our version of happiness.

Just to reinforce this: my philosophy is about you finding your version of happiness, not your mother's version, your husband's, or your best friend's—your unique version of what happiness is to you. Then you can start living it.

Many people have the best intentions at the beginning of a new year to do things differently and achieve more. Yet how many excuses did you use last year that prevented you from achieving those goals and desires? You don't have to become a better person or develop a different attitude to have a life you love and find happiness. As you are, you are good enough.

Hello Coach!

I believe there is intense pressure in today's adrenaline-fueled society—we all get a constant barrage of societal messages telling us how to live our lives, what to wear, what to say, what not to say, what not to wear, the type of house we should have, the suburb we must live in, the type of car we must drive. The message is all the same: "If you're not happy with it, get rid of it! Don't worry about the consequences, live for today!"

I believe that this mode of existence contributes toward anxiety, depression, and other illnesses because it creates so much stress, disillusionment, and a lack of inner peace and fulfillment. But before we go any further, I just want to make things really clear by emphasizing these three points:

First, your happiness starts right here. My job is to guide you to find out who you are in that picture of happiness, then help you put steps in place so you can start living it. I have no intention of dragging you into some program that tells you to stand up and be a different person. Life just isn't that simple, and wishful thinking and affirmations alone won't make it so. I don't think people solve problems with just positive thinking either.

Second, propping up your thoughts or pretending to feel differently than you really do is not a sturdy enough system for the long haul. Creative visualizations are limited too. I've met a lot of people who can't visualize and others who feel strongly conflicted even imagining what they love. And trendy phrases such as "create your own reality" sound empowering but the flip side is that you can end up blaming yourself for everything that goes wrong. That's not fair. You're not big enough to take on fate single-handedly, and you don't need to.

Third, for many people, if we are not feeling great about what we look like, we often try and find external relief by buying a new dress, getting a new boyfriend, moving into a new house, getting a new car, and so on. These are all quick fixes and never sustain the feeling we desire: true love and acceptance for ourselves and who we are.

A person who has a healthy relationship with themselves is not defined by how they look or what material possessions they have. People who live with purpose are generally happier and feel more successful; they also remember to put time in just for themselves.

When I take a look at how I actually practice happiness in my daily life, it all starts with gratitude. Before I even put my feet on the floor in the morning, I lie in bed and think of all the things in my life that bring me joy, and sometimes the things that don't particularly bring me joy but that I'm still grateful for because of the lessons that they bring me.

Then I pray. It might take two minutes, it might take a little longer, but I roll through my practice of gratitude and into prayer and then I set the intention for the feeling that I want to experience throughout the day, the feeling that I want aligned in my head, heart, and body. That might translate to me visualizing the meeting that I'm having later that day, the feeling I will be having during the meeting, the outcome of that meeting, what I want to say during that meeting. It all plays out like a movie in my head.

My morning routine will find me with a cup of tea in hand and some quiet time spent in mindfulness and meditation. Sitting and connecting to God in this way allows me to really hear myself clearly and with compassion. It also allows me to go about my day with calm and awareness.

I really try to go through most of my days in a state of mindfulness. It's not always easy and time has taught me some tricks to reducing stress when I find myself too busy or overloaded. If I'm having a really hectic day with lots of meetings, I'll make time to find a nearby park or beach and take ten minutes out to just reconnect to myself and calm my mind. Sometimes I'll arrive early to a meeting and sit in the car quietly meditating on the intention that I have for that meeting. I've also learned the hard way that not overbooking my diary is one of the keys to reduce stress, and therefore promote happiness, in my life.

I also end my days the same way that I start them. I reflect back on the day that has passed with gratitude, prayers of thankfulness, and meditation. It's through my consistent daily commitment to gratitude, mindfulness, prayer, intention setting, and meditation that I find peace, positivity, and happiness. And when I don't do these things, I literally feel like I'm starved of vital nutrients, that I'm out of sync with myself on every level and quite disoriented. Things aren't effortless or easy and I don't enjoy the seasick feeling of misalignment. Basically, I miss my happiness and serenity and I just try really hard not to let that happen.

As you embark on the following tasks, I'd like you to remember that you're trying to identify your version of happiness. Don't think about anyone else during this process. Just you.

Task 1: Things that make you feel happy

Create a daily or weekly checklist of all the things you want to do, yet feel you don't have time for. Then make sure you do at least one thing on this list each week until you reach the end of the list.

Don't censor this list.

You may want to play a game of tennis each week, have a regular catch-up with a girlfriend over a cuppa, sit in the sun and read a book, or treat yourself to a soothing aromatherapy massage.

Or maybe you want to meditate each morning before you start your day, or have a soak in the bath with lots of bubbles and a glass of wine, listening to your favorite music instead of watching television every night.

All of these things are valid. The point is just don't take life (or this list) too seriously.

The things that make me feel good are:

1. _____

2. _____

3. _____

Task 2: The balance checklist

Identify as many things as you can that make you feel wonderful and nourish your soul. If you're not taking time out for yourself to recharge your batteries on a regular basis, you can become frustrated and irritable.

The checklist below focuses on giving time and attention to you. Our relationship with ourselves primarily shapes who we are and can add meaning to other areas of our lives. You are important. Make the time to make *you* a priority.

Hello Coach!

Put T (True) of F (False) next to these points, and throughout the course of your program, make a commitment to work on the areas that you marked F.

- I spend time doing the things I love to do.
- I have nourishing relationships.
- I believe I can support myself:
    - financially
    - physically
    - emotionally
    - spiritually.
- I feel happy with my appearance.
- I visit the dentist, optometrist, and doctor for regular check-ups (or other health professionals that you consult with such as acupuncturists, naturopaths, chiropractors, etc.).
- I have at least three holidays and/or breaks per year.
- I eat healthy foods.
- I leave work at work.
- I communicate my feelings honestly.
- I make time for physical exercise.
- I don't have any outstanding issues that need resolving.
- I treat myself each week to something I enjoy.
- I easily say no and cancel non-urgent appointments.
- I laugh with my friends each week.
- I surround myself with things I consider to be beautiful.
- I feel calm and focused.
- I have high energy.
- I tell the people in my life that I love them daily.

Task 3: Making time

Book a date with yourself—for the next six months, you need to block out time in your diary just for you to do whatever you want.

Increase the amount of time you allocate from month to month. If you start with an hour a week, increase it each week by another hour (using your common sense as to how much time you can spare).

Although there will be times you may need to rearrange these days to suit, set a schedule that honors you by limiting potential interruptions. This time spent disconnecting from the world and focusing on yourself can have a profound effect upon your mood.

Your affirmation for happiness

"I create my own happiness and I take time out to love me."

Your daily task

Every day is a new day, and during your process of change, you need to be vigilant about continuing to do the things that will bring about change. One of the most important components to this is the daily "mind chatter" dump. Just a quick reminder. No one needs to see this, and it doesn't need to make sense to anyone but you. This is the cleansing ritual to start your day and create space for the positive thoughts to begin to flow in.

Your review

1. What were my personal highlights during this happiness phase?
2. What challenges did I face and how did I handle them?
3. What exciting new insights did I discover about myself?
4. What was my greatest achievement in this phase?
5. What is my commitment for the next phase?

Remember

By the end of this book, you will discover what inspires you and who you want to be—and then you'll achieve it.

Your checklist

A. Complete Task 1: Things that make you feel happy.
B. Complete Task 2: The balance checklist.
C. Complete Task 3: Making time.
D. Write out affirmation and verbalize daily.
E. Your daily task: "mind chatter" dump.
F. Complete review.

YOUR LIFE'S PURPOSE

This chapter concentrates on the most exciting and uplifting topic of your unique purpose. I fundamentally believe that you were born with a magnificent, one-of-a-kind purpose and awakening that is why we are here.

When we reignite the purpose that we all have within us, use it to the best of our ability, and the betterment of ourselves and others, we truly are living a life of inspiration. Not only are we doing soul nourishing work, we are finding our way to true fulfillment within ourselves.

Every day that I work with new clients, I hear versions of the same claim: people saying that they don't know or understand what their true purpose is, and they don't know how to get there. But experience has taught me that this is not true. I say to them, "In your heart, you know exactly what you would love to do, but the guilt and fear in your head stops you from acknowledging it." It's difficult to step away from the guilt and fear that we carry around and acknowledge our true desires. It's confronting and uncomfortable. However, living with the gnawing sensation of ignoring our true desires is so much worse, and indeed limiting, than admitting our heart's passion. Once we understand it's only our internal fear-based monologue that is holding us back and we vocalize our purpose, we can begin to feel more connected to ourselves and our lives.

I knew for a very long time what my life's purpose was before I actually identified it. I knew I wanted to help people heal, probably because I knew that I somehow needed to heal myself. I'd been on a quest my whole life seeking answers to the pain that I was feeling, and that I most definitely needed to eradicate from my life. What I struggled with until I found coaching were the tools to actually do the healing.

I remember the exact moment that I realized what my purpose was. I was in a hotel room in the US, partway through a coaching course, when I realized that this was it. My heart was thudding in my chest. I was filled with a sense of knowing that I had found my answer. None of this is to say that I literally had it all together right there and then, but the door to the future was opened up enough for me to know where I had to step next, and that was a career dedicated to coaching because it would give me all the equipment that I needed to help the people that would come to me, looking to become the best possible versions of themselves. I was really clear—my life's purpose was to help people, and coaching was the mechanism in which to do it. The relief, bliss, and utter joy at uncovering this knowledge and seeing the path forward made me feel lighter.

I truly believe that uncovering one's life purpose isn't as difficult and complex as many people make it out to be. When I walk into a client's home, I can tell a lot about them from the books they're reading, the way they decorate, the things that they're interested in, the things they talk about that light them up from the inside. I can also tell a lot about a person from the timeline of their lives: what they've been doing, who they've been spending time with, where they've been spending their time, and so on. All these clues shine a light on what a client's passions might be and those passions, more often than not, tell me a lot about what a person's life purpose may be. And my experience tells me that passion and purpose are very closely allied. You can't have purpose without passion, and you can't have passion without purpose.

Even when we do have our purpose and passions aligned, the road might not always be the easiest to navigate. Sometimes knowing with deep intuitiveness what we're meant to do in the world can bring us a multitude of hurdles to overcome and we find ourselves not only questioning our path but also our commitment to it, and even at times our own sanity.

And of even greater frustration to some people that I've worked with is the journey to uncovering their talents and purpose. Sometimes trying to reveal them can be hard work in and of itself. But the talents, gifts, and passions are always there in someone's life; it just requires a bit of time and effort to uncover them.

Going through the exercises in this book will help you to shed the clutter and noise around you that might have hidden your passions and purpose. Understanding your unique skills and strengths helps identify and crystallize your passion and connects you to your life's purpose.

I'm incredibly passionate about helping people create revenue streams from what they're passionate about. My philosophy around one's life purpose is that if you have gifts that you're aware of and bring passion to your life, how do we connect those passions to your purpose, and how can we use those purposes and passions to make the world a better place?

I truly believe that we're here to make the world a better place. It's a quaint, somewhat old-fashioned notion, sure, but without helping humankind to be better, whatever that looks like, we all face a level of existential crisis. And we just don't need to. If we take a good look at the global COVID-19 pandemic of 2020–1, I think that most of us would agree that this has been an crisis that has stopped many people dead in their tracks. It's got them thinking about what they really want to do with their lives.

I've certainly had many more clients come to me to facilitate life changes, changes that have been instigated by the pain of the pandemic and the experience of the fragility of life. It's been wonderful to be able to help these people, but it's also been crushing to see the scale of the devastation. However, I do believe that we are all looking at a shift toward kindness and respect and a move away from the more shadowy aspects of ourselves. And that can only be for the better.

The bottom line is that we all have a life purpose, we can discover and act upon it, and I'm here to help you do that. It's not hard, but it does require some commitment and a bit of work. Your purpose is something that is innately yours, something that no one can do better than you and when you do it, your heart soars. But what stops us from verbally expressing this purpose is, simply, fear. F. E. A. R. stands for Forgetting Everything is All Right.

Your purpose

When I start to explore the notion of purpose with my clients, they usually come up with similar responses that include:

- I'm not good enough.
- I'm no one special.
- I don't have any special gifts.
- I don't have anything special to contribute to the world.

Those statements and beliefs are simply not true. They are wrong. And if you believe any of those things, you're wrong too! These are simply beliefs built up over a period of time that have embedded themselves in your day-to-day thought processes and need to be stopped. You are a unique individual with unique talents that no one else has.

In life, remember, you are here for a reason. That reason may be that you are meant to be a fantastic mother and that's what makes your heart sing, or it may be to build an empire that changes the world economy. Whatever your purpose is, own it, because it's yours. You may not know the details yet, but your soul is waiting for you to call on it. So, start with what you know. Your purpose is never outside of you, it is always inside, and it is something you already know. Do what you know. Develop what you know and what inspires you.

Why is purpose so important?

Searching for meaning in life is an eternal, universal phenomenon. No matter how busy we may become with our weekly schedules, for many people worldwide there is often a sense of longing. This longing is at times a feeling that something important to our life's ultimate goal just can't be pinned down. Many of my clients report that no matter how "fulfilled" they may be in many exterior measures of "success," they often still feel a lingering, haunting sense that their true purpose in life is unclear.

The desire to self-actualize and to fulfill all aspects of our ultimate potential is in fact a very real human need. We are all born wondering deep down what our life's purpose actually is and we are bound to continue to feel restless, and at times deeply dissatisfied, until we find it.

Psychologists such as Carl Jung have identified repeatedly that our subconscious longings are the key to knowing our real purpose in life. On a day-to-day level, our conscious minds can tend to crowd and overwhelm our perception about what our subconscious mind is trying to reveal to us. We are given constant clues through dreams and unshakable gut feelings as to what we are really here to do—our true purpose—but our brain can muddy our sight by using messaging, such as "I don't know if I can do that", "I'm not sure I'm special enough", "I am not good enough", etc. to stop us from deeply engaging with our core beliefs and internal understanding of ourselves and thus push us further and further from our purpose.

It's taken me over twenty years of honing my craft, strengthening my inner voice, and solidifying my purpose and using the tools that I believe in to arrive at the place that I am now, which is deep into the development and launch of my global coaching platform, Hello Coach. I am quite happy to tell you that I've struggled with self-doubt for many years, but I have also known that I have the tools and the knowledge to support myself through those dark times of doubt, and it's imperative that I share them.

My natural and intuitive pull toward wanting to help people lead better lives resulted in me becoming a life coach. All the experiences that I went through guided me toward my career: the ups the downs, the successes, the disappointments, the wins, the losses—all of it. And what I have come to realize from my journey is that change can come from one of two places: pain or pleasure. Things are so bad that we have to change because we find we can no longer live in the chaos. Or things are so good that we want to create more of that feeling and we are motivated by the good times.

Being willing and able to identify exactly what one's true purpose is in life is of utmost importance to our ultimate fulfillment. For the human psyche, it's as essential as breathing, and ignoring this yearning for meaning sets us up for continuous longing and frustration.

If you are still questioning whether you are living your purpose or don't understand why you are feeling empty inside, review the questions below and check in with yourself to give yourself the inspiration to move—and move on.

Task 1: Reflection

Would you agree or disagree with the following statements?

- I often feel unenthusiastic about going to work.
- I have often wondered if there was more for me out there.
- I like my work but feel my talents are wasted.
- My real meaning comes in the things that are outside my work.
- I want to be really passionate about what I do with my life, not just going through the motions.
- I want to feel that I have made a difference with my life.

If you agreed with more than one of these statements, it is time to create an action plan and get you living a life of purpose and passion.

Task 2: Something unique about you

Many people think that when we find what our life's purpose is, it will bring untold peace, happiness, and joy into our lives, but rarely do we see that unfold. We overcomplicate things by asking ourselves other questions, such as "What am I meant to be doing?", "What job will keep me satisfied?", or statements like "I will eventually be happy when I find my life's purpose, but until then I don't know what it is!"

All these common questions are asked by thousands of people every day, yet we often fail to see the signs along our own unique path, guiding us right to the answers we seek to discover what our life's purpose is. After all, isn't the point of existence ultimately about pushing through the boundaries of the everyday and seeking to unleash the extraordinary that is within each of us?

I can't overstate the importance of identifying your personal destiny because the essence of this element of your life forms the core of your personality and day-to-day behaviors.

Before I discovered my own purpose, I remember spending my teenage years and early twenties feeling pretty lost, despite my efforts at trying to figure out who I was. I didn't land on my purpose until I'd had my son and experienced coaching for myself. Coaching helped me quantify and put into an actual statement what my purpose was. It took me working with a coach to understand how I could use my life's experiences and training to live a life I loved.

This highlights my idea that sometimes you don't need to immediately know what your life's purpose is but following the path of your passions can actually help reveal to you your life's purpose.

When we follow the path of least resistance, our purpose in life can't help but show up. Pursuing the things that make us happy and keep us in a state of joy also keeps us aligned to our true nature, feeding our minds, bodies, and souls.

Harnessing and understanding your gifts, passions, and purpose is the fun part of life; it can light up your life and create genuine happiness. If it's possible to create an income stream from your passion and purpose, this is great too, but doing so isn't mandatory to finding fulfillment; it's just an added bonus.

Doing the things in our life that truly fuel our being can keep us buoyant when the times are tough and challenges arise. Life is like that; it will throw curveballs at you when you least expect it. But following the path of your gifts and passions will never let you down. Life taking you on the meandering path, rather than the most direct route to your purpose, is not wrong; it's just the long way round. However, where there is a lack of joy, happiness, bliss, and passion, that is the wrong path, it is not in alignment, and the signs will be obvious. Your energy will be low, your motivation will be non-existent, and you'll find rain clouds where there should be sunshine. It will quite simply be overall discomfort in every aspect of your life and being.

Choosing to do the work of shedding limiting beliefs and trusting in our gifts and passions will lead us to our purpose, and toward a life that elevates not only ourselves but those we share the planet with too.

Everything, from your choice of job to your partners, to friendships and even your taste in books, clothes, and music, are informed by your ultimate destiny in life. Our job right here, right now, is to help you locate it, name it, and claim it.

I believe that we all have gifts that are unique and personal to us as individuals, yet many of us who are yearning or longing for satisfaction have misjudged our gifts by either ignoring them, undervaluing them, or not recognizing them for what they are: the actual component in our lives that sets us apart and make us special.

Discovering what makes your heart sing when you do it—creating beautiful art, making people laugh, being a sensational cook, being an exceptional listener, awesome lover, great athlete (the list is endless)—and true acceptance of that unique gift is the ultimate key to life and quite simply nothing short of a magical unmasking of your true self.

Your task here is to ask yourself the following questions in this order:

What is it that you bring to life that is special about you and adds a contribution to the planet and to your life? Then, spend time really noticing what it is for you.

Extend this exercise by answering the following questions:

- What is it you bring to your family?
- What is it you bring to work?
- What is it you bring to your partnerships and friendships?

The answers may be different but there will most likely be a theme. Pay attention to that theme.

Discover who you are

Write down the answers to the following in your journal or notebook:

- What do you love about yourself?
- What makes you special and unique?
- If your mom, partner, and best friend were to tell you five things that make you special, what would they be? Ask them to give you feedback.
- How often are you being who you love to be?
- In what areas of your life do you get to be the beautiful version of who you are, and where and with whom do you not allow this to shine?
- Acknowledge yourself daily—write down five things that you want to acknowledge yourself for.
- What are your gifts?
- Why are you here?
- What are you passionate about?

Write a press release or social media post about living your life's purpose

Write a press release or social media post that's all about you. What does your ideal day look like? Write a description of the perfect day in the life of you. Read back over your vision and print it out or save it to your phone. The key here is to place it somewhere where you can read it each day and remind yourself of your desire to live your purpose.

Answering the following questions will help you to write a post or press release about yourself. Remember when answering that you love yourself one hundred percent.

- How do you feel about your appearance?
- How do you interact with others?
- How do others treat you?
- What hours do you work?
- How do you nourish your energy, body, and mind?
- How do you act with colleagues, family, and friends?
- How do you react to negative comments and situations?
- What do you choose to eat for meals?
- Describe the special time you spend with yourself every day.

Here's a sample press release/social media post:

It's March and I wake up every day and look at the beach. I am so excited to start my day as a florist. I have thirteen clients and my business is growing each week. I style beautiful homes with amazing flowers. I love going to the flower markets each day and choosing unique flowers for my clients. I love that my home is continually filled with the scent of fresh flowers.

I wear casual yet chic clothes and it feels amazing to not have to wear a suit. I keep my own hours in my business, and it allows me time to study and have free time to develop my skills and have fun. No matter what anyone says to me, I believe in my dream and I am living it!

Create an action plan

Create an action plan of when you are going to start living your unique purpose.

If your purpose is to work with flowers and you have secretly desired owning your own florist's shop, and you want to decorate beautiful homes and bring happiness to yourself and those around you, then start being an example of this.

Start your action plan out by stating a simple goal, such as the one below, then move through the questions and start formulating your action plan. Writing this information down will help bring into alignment the many thoughts swirling through your head right now and aid in formulating some clear structure for identifying your life's purpose.

A goal is a stated aim. When we set goals, we lay out our desired results. In order to achieve those goals, we attach steps on how to get there. This is an action plan. It's essentially a road map that guides us from the point where we are now to our goal somewhere in the future. Carefully plotting out the steps it will take to attain our goal not only keeps us organized, accountable, and focused, but also helps us to clearly see any issues that may arise and require us to pivot or make changes to our plan to achieve our goal. The more detailed we can be at this point in our journey, the clearer we become on what it is that we are striving to do.

I've outlined some key points that will help guide you into making an action plan. Not all of them will be applicable to your goal; however, they are meant to spark some ideas and give you some guidelines for things to consider.

Sample goal

I love styling flowers and decorating homes in a way that brings happiness to others. By the end of October, I am creating beautiful flowers for beautiful homes and have a successful, thriving business.

Sample action plan

Write a vision of your ideal day. Here are some questions to help you visualize your ideal day: a) Is it a new business or a part-time weekend job? b) What is it I want to create? c) what do I need to get this started?

1. Approach three places and inquire about possible opportunities to donate my time to a florist's shop to gain experience.

2. Inquire about any floristry courses that could help improve my skills.

3. Approach friends and ask if they know someone who could benefit from my new business idea.

4. Write my detailed business plan. (If your goal is to create a new business, or realign one that's not quite where you want it, start at the beginning.) My business plan focuses on how much money I'll need to get started, what my expenses will look like, who my vendors etc. might be. I will make an appointment with a financial planner or an accountant to help me, or use the internet to research this and see what information comes to light. (Even just a cursory browse around your subject matter will bring up

some information that you probably hadn't thought about and most likely will ignite some great new thoughts and ideas.)

5. Create a vision board of my life's purpose by cutting out pictures of everything I wish to create and ask my higher power to provide. I visualize this daily and imagine my success. I look at my vision board and see myself experiencing all that I have on my vision board.

6. Declutter. I get rid of what I do not want. This will make room for what I *do* want in my life and create the space for it to come in. I can declutter clothes, people, furniture, debts, home, negative thoughts, and an unfulfilling job. (I cannot stress the importance of ridding yourself of things that are impeding your advancement. If it's in your way, it is not helping you. Be strong and get rid of the roadblocks.)

7. Work with a life coach. Working with a coach will help me discover my life's purpose and what my gifts are. (Studies have shown conclusively that people who take responsibility for their own lives, who have a sense of being in control of their life, are happier, healthier, and ultimately more likely to achieve overall success.)

Task 3: Identifying your life's purpose

If you're clear about your life's purpose, you'll find yourself overflowing with enthusiasm, energy, and excitement for your future to unfold. Getting out of bed and facing each day with unbridled joy, gratitude, and inspiration will propel you forward with little effort because you know exactly what you're meant to be doing. None of this is to say that you won't face hard work getting there, but that work will be satisfying because you're working toward achieving your life's purpose.

Let's start to really drill down into your life's purpose by answering the following questions in your journal.

1. What are the five things I most want in my life?
2. What five changes do I want to see on the planet that I'm passionate about?
3. What five things make me special and unique?
4. What five things can I do and love to do now?

Then choose a favorite answer from each question and, in order, slot the answers into the following sentence:

"I will create [answer from question 1], using my [answer from question 2], to accomplish [answer to question 3] and also achieve [answer to question 4]."

The resulting statement will give you a very clear indication as to your life's purpose.

Your affirmation for finding your purpose

"I know my purpose and live my purpose every day."

Your daily must-do

Time for that daily "mind chatter" dump. By now, you should start to recognize the benefits of creating the space for positivity to flow in by letting go of all the thinking that doesn't serve you.

Your review

1. What were my personal highlights during this purpose phase?
2. What challenges did I face and how did I handle them?
3. What exciting new insights did I discover about myself?
4. What was my greatest achievement in this phase?
5. What is my commitment for the next phase?

Remember

By the end of this book, you will discover what inspires you and who you want to be—and then you'll achieve it.

Your checklist

A. Complete Task 1: Reflection.
B. Complete Task 2: Something unique about you.
C. Complete Task 3: Identifying your life's purpose.
D. Write out affirmation and verbalize daily.
E. Your daily task: "mind chatter" dump.
F. Complete review.

CREATING YOUR VISION

If you don't spend time creating and designing what is truly in your heart and what you actually want for your life—your vision—then life and circumstances will create your vision for you and that will mean you have less control over the vision, and therefore your life. You'll be essentially the passenger in the car rather than the driver. You'll get to a destination but you'll have had no input into what you saw or witnessed along the way; the ride will just have washed over you.

You can't change what life throws at you; however, by creating and designing your life, you have ultimate control over how you respond to that. I believe that you need to have a master plan for your life, so you know where you're going to end up. Sure, life comes in and you can go with the flow, trusting in fate. However, you need to have a clear vision of what you want to create for your life and allow that to blend with your trust.

It's like making a cake. Before you start baking, you need to be aware of the ingredients necessary to create the cake. Similarly, you need to know what's required to create your vision. Knowing who you are, what you value, what you believe in—and being totally committed to, and doing, everything it takes to get there—is key.

One of the most important aspects of the creation of the vision for your life is simply sitting still and identifying what you think is currently missing from your life. This task shouldn't be too difficult for most people. It's easy enough to look at our daily lives and say we are unhappy about certain things: our job, our paycheck, our house, our partner, our friends. When all the elements that go toward defining happiness are not quite right, or simply not even there, we all feel a sense of unease and discord. We know elementally that things just aren't right and we're uncomfortable.

When I had the opportunity to create a new vision of what I wanted in my own life, it was pretty simple. I'd just left my first marriage with a suitcase, enough money in the bank to last me three months, and my son. My needs were: find a place to live, find clients for my new coaching business, and make enough money to feed myself and my son. That was it.

I found a tiny two-bedroom house to rent with a studio/office out the back and I sat down and figured out that I needed to see ten clients a week at $100 per session to be able to afford my living expenses. In those days, there was no social media, no websites to set up; it was old school relationship-building and getting to know people who were going to get me clients. I visited all the doctors' offices, wellness centers, chiropractors, and massage therapists in the area, introduced myself, and said I would be willing to give a VIP talk on the benefits of coaching for free. It took a couple of weeks, but by the end of that time I had the ten clients, and I was on my way. Incidentally, my whole coaching business has relied on word-of-mouth referrals to attract clients. The Universe really did deliver when I needed it to.

As I moved through the next twenty years of life, I've come back to this exercise time and time again about finding my vision and working through the practices in the book to create a road map to achieve it. The point here is that this is not a one-and-done drill; this is a life lesson that can be repeated over and over again.

Finding your vision

Perhaps even now, you're sitting here reading this book and asking yourself, "What do I want for my life?" or "How do I want to live my life?" or "Am I living my life by other people's values or by mine?"

These are all important, valid questions. And it's also important for you to know that it's only when you seek the truth of how you want to live your life—and not live by the rules and expectations of others—that you can begin to set yourself free and create a life that honors you.

It's critically important to understand that examining the things that are not sitting well with you and leaving you feeling inadequate and discouraged is a positive, compassionate, and brave step forward. People tend to put off self-examination precisely because it is hard, and we generally are our own harshest critics, but shining the light on the stuff that we're not happy about and committing to finding ways to improve and change those things can only make our lives better. Becoming clear on how you want your life to be is the most important step to take! If you don't take control of your life and your desires, life will control it for you and you will always be accountable to others instead of yourself. If you don't get clear on how you want to fill your days, others will fill your days for you.

Your story

So, what is it that you want to create for your life?

There is no universal version of success or failure; there is only what is right as decided by you. The tasks in this chapter will help you listen to what *your* needs are—not what others live their lives by—and bring clarity to things that will serve you in creating a life that you love.

We often judge one another based on our definition of success, which is limiting for ourselves as well as those we judge. One person may feel successful if they have a husband, two kids, a job, and own their own home. Another person may believe that their personal vision is to earn two million dollars a year. For someone else, it may be a vision to have a balanced life or to be a loving and generous person. Regardless of what you desire, it's important to understand what your vision is and then identify how you can make it a reality.

Do you often wonder why some people are successful, yet others seem to struggle each day? Perhaps it's because those who are living their version of success and happiness were committed to finding it. Most people who reach all-time high points in life have embarked on an intense process of self-discovery and change to make their dreams a reality. They have done the work of reflecting on toxic patterns which were preventing them from living a life they loved. This is hard work—creating change is hard—but it's work you need to do if you want to have the life of your dreams. If you stay stuck in the same routines and patterns, it's most likely that life will stay the same.

If you embark upon change and take consistent action toward your dreams, it's more than likely they will become reality.

Even just writing down your dreams and goals gives you more of a chance to succeed than not doing anything.

While you are working on creating your vision, remember to spend as much time on the doing as on the being. That is, carve out a balance between resting and relaxing, and taking action and being busy.

I personally find it easier to think about doing and being as masculine and feminine. Doing exercises are things like making our lists, moving things forward through creation, meetings, basically some kind of propulsion forward, and to my mind those things fall into the category of the masculine side of us. The feminine, or being, side of us is made up of things such as meditation, mindfulness, prayer, contemplation. It's the quieter practices that tend to make us more introspective and thoughtful and require less physical output.

As an example, I tend to start my day in the feminine energy, with my gratitude practice, prayer, and meditation. Then as I roll through my day my energy patterns shift toward more masculine pursuits; meetings, phone calls, creating plans, and business strategies for future projects. I'll circle back to my more feminine energy as I end my day with prayer and meditation.

It's taken me many years to find a balance between the feminine and the masculine in my day-to-day; however, I've learned that it's vitally important to do so, because a little too much either way will make me feel overwhelmed and fatigued. I'll end up with my heart racing, a headache, and just a general feeling of overload. I don't like it, and quite frankly, it's simply not worth it to me anymore because I find I don't make my best decisions, or operate from my best, most thoughtful position, when I'm feeling overloaded. So, I strive for balance as much as I can every day.

You must find time to create peace and fulfillment as you embark on this journey of creating success and transformation in your life.

Task 1: The My Life Wheel

Review the My Life Wheel below and decide where you want to devote time and energy in your new life.

The objective of reviewing this wheel is to check in with yourself and ask yourself how satisfied you are in these areas of your life.

First: consider all the areas of your life that are important to you. (In the next chapter, we will create goals and intentions that reflect what you want after completing these exercises.)

- Career
- Family
- Friends/social/fun
- Financial
- Home
- Health
- Spirituality
- Love
- Recreation
- Self-image.

Second: draw a line through the areas you are satisfied with. These are not the areas you need to focus on for the purposes of this exercise: it's the areas you aren't satisfied with that form the background to the following step.

Third: ask yourself some questions:

1. What do I want?
2. Is this what I really want?
3. What's preventing me from putting time into this area?
4. What is the smallest step I can do that puts me in the direction of what I want?
5. Review this area regularly.

Task 2: A Day in the Life of Me

Write out "A Day in the Life of Me" and do it with one hundred percent love, compassion, and respect for, and acceptance of, yourself. It should be a day in the life of you living the life you want because this is your script for life. Remember you must love yourself one hundred percent when answering these questions—anything less and you won't really be writing about the life you want.

Your scenario does not have to be very long if you're not comfortable writing a lot. It should be as long as it needs to be for you to fully describe the Day in the Life you really want to have.

Consider the following when writing your scenario:

1. How do you feel about your appearance?
2. How do you greet others?
3. How do others treat you?
4. How do you act with colleagues, family, and friends?
5. Describe how you share your love for the world.
6. What does your day look like?
7. How are you spending your day?
8. How do you react to negative comments and situations?
9. What foods do you fuel your body with?
10. Describe the nourishing time you spend with yourself every day.
11. How do you express thanks to your God (your version of God) or The Universe each day?

A Day in the Life of Me example

It's January, two years into the future. I wake each day and I love my life. I have the career I have dreamed about, and I am in a loving relationship that inspires me.

I eat healthy, wholesome foods and I go for walks on the beach each morning. I have a balanced lifestyle that makes me smile each day.

I spend time with friends each week and have a dedicated hour each week that I attend meditation classes with some of my friends. I feel relaxed and joyful and energized about meeting every day with poise and grace.

Task 3: Accomplishments

While you work through this book, from time to time I will ask you to reflect on and check in with your achievements—both major and day-to-day— to remind you to recognize and celebrate these achievements.

It's important to observe all your wins along the way, no matter how small or large. One of the ways to get to know you again is to start validating yourself. Start to learn that you are important and what you do, as well as who you are, deserves recognition on a daily basis.

I invite you to do the following exercise in your journal each week.

My five most important accomplishments this week were the following:

Achievement 1: _____

Achievement 2: _____

Achievement 3: _____

Achievement 4: _____

Achievement 5: _____

Your daily must-do

I know that at the end of each chapter, I am reminding you to get rid of all the negative thoughts ahead of the new day. It's a way of reminding you to create a habit in which you are consciously focusing on ridding your mind of negative thoughts and allowing space for all the positive that life has to offer to enter into your mental space and create that reality. "Mind chatter" dump away!

Your review

1. What were my personal highlights during this vision phase?
2. What challenges did I face and how did I handle them?
3. What exciting new insights did I discover about myself?
4. What was my greatest achievement in this phase?
5. What is my commitment for the next phase?

Your affirmation for creating your vision

"I'm attracting new opportunities each and every day."

Remember

By the end of this book, you will discover what inspires you and who you want to be—and then you'll achieve it.

Your checklist

A. Complete Task 1: The My Life Wheel.
B. Complete Task 2: A Day in the Life of Me.
C. Complete Task 3: Accomplishments.
D. Write out affirmation and verbalize daily.
E. Your daily task: "mind chatter" dump.
F. Complete review.

SETTING YOUR GOAL

I often ask clients the question, "If you had the opportunity to attempt anything you could in life, and not fail, would you do it?" This question underpins my ideas around goal setting and provides a critical base of no fear, no second-guessing, and no boundaries when approaching this activity. That unspoken dream that you've held close to your heart that you've never uttered to anyone, the thing, or things, as you might have a couple of ideas that you can't stop thinking about when you let your mind wander, but you then let that negative side of yourself say: too hard, too much money, not good enough, not enough time, etc.—these are aspects of your life that we want to get to, and in doing so, formulate a plan to get you there.

I can vividly recall my nervousness and excitement as I prepared to meet with my coach all those years ago. I was way outside of my comfort zone, but I was determined to find a new direction in life, no matter what. I was a new mom, with a gaping hole in my life where I knew happiness should be, but wasn't.

That first conversation was an eye-opener. My coach helped me clarify and articulate what it was that I was struggling with—my desire to build a new, happy life that provided me with stability, fulfillment, and purpose. It was so simple; I needed a plan that was thorough, achievable, and based on my needs. I needed willingness and commitment to reaching my goals.

Finally, after years of ad hoc searching and trying to find new ways of being, I had a conversation with someone who provided me with the techniques to see an endpoint and the means to get there. This was the modality that truly resonated with me and was going to move me from a place of frustration to a place of empowerment. At last, I knew where I was going.

During this chapter, you may find yourself struggling with your self-definition. The tools and exercises may seem challenging, and you may want to stop here. Remember that this is part of the process. Changing your perception of yourself can be exciting and hard. Letting go of the old is part of making space for the new. If in doubt, review the contract you made with yourself at the start.

Setting goals is important. Having a goal means that you have thought about something that you want to achieve and have your mind set on doing so. Goal setting focuses your mind to track and measure the actions that allow you to reach your goal. If you feel that you're going off the path to your goal, or missing some steps in getting there, having a goal allows you to reassess during your journey and correct anything that isn't working for you.

One of the most important things you'll do in this process is create a master plan. Beyond setting a goal, we're looking at creating a plan for your life. If that means tweaking one area of your life for which you want to create one goal, or it means completely transforming your life as you know it and making ten goals, the master plan is the crucial point that you start from.

Keep your goals short, measurable, achievable, realistic, and put a time frame on them. I'm also going to ask you to write them down because the power of writing down a goal is as powerful as then manifesting it. Clarity is the key. You need to note down your goal succinctly in a precise, short phrase or sentence.

If you don't have any goals, you are quite simply at the mercy of life and all that it can throw at you. Without goals, you become a rudderless boat in a surging ocean that will, at some point, run into the rocks and be smashed to smithereens. Basically, you'll end up being so frustrated by the control that is being exerted upon you from circumstances, people, and events, that you'll find yourself articulating in no uncertain terms: "I just want this to be different!"

When I made my goals, there was no doubt that I felt like I was getting back in control of my life. I had left my marriage, I had found a new home, I had begun my coaching business, and I was a single parent to a beautiful baby boy. I felt like I had some guardrails up to guide my progression forward but I also knew that new dreams and desires and needs and wants would come up in my life and I'd have to reassess my goals and the ways in which I needed to address and achieve them.

There are a couple of thoughts to keep in mind around goal setting that I find particularly helpful not only to me, but for my clients as well. First, when you're setting your goals have a time frame in mind for each one. That could be a day, a week, a month, a year, whatever is applicable to the goal. Recognize that you need a little flexibility with these time frames. Life will happen and there are times that you need to roll with it, but don't give up just because you've missed a self-imposed deadline. Look at that deadline realistically and see if you can't amend it to be more appropriate.

Second, celebrate the wins! If you've set yourself a goal to walk for twenty minutes every day for a month to increase your health, do something special for yourself at the end of the month before setting the next health goal, which might be to run every day for fifteen minutes for a whole month. Celebrating the wins will motivate us to tackle more challenging goals.

Third, and this is one that I'm super passionate about, write it down. Research suggests that writing down our goals tends to make them more achievable, not to mention it gets us really clear on what we're focusing on.

Recently, I found myself sitting on a few extra COVID pounds that weren't making me feel great. I was lethargic and uncomfortable in my own body. I realized that I needed to stop, assess the situation, and create a goal around changing where I found myself.

I wasn't necessarily looking to lose weight, but I was focused on feeling stronger and more grounded within myself. I've found that as I get older, the muscle tone needs a little more attention, a little more love. So, I sat down and created a plan to reach my goal of seeing muscle definition in my arms and legs within two months. There it was, my goal and the time frame in which I wanted to achieve it.

The steps to getting there looked like this: I would walk every day for forty-five minutes, then I'd come home and do a thirty-minute workout including weights, cardio, and sit-ups. I also decided to train at Crossfit three times a week and pay extra attention to my diet, eating cleansing, nutritious food, and be on top of my water intake.

I knew that I'd need to align my thoughts with my actions, so I added in a daily affirmation: "I love seeing and feeling my body becoming healthier and stronger." My mindset was supporting my actions, which were supporting my goals. This was a pretty straightforward health goal, but achieving a goal propagates the idea that if you can achieve this goal, you can also achieve others. It's pretty simple, and I like to break complex things down to simple, achievable tasks so that I can stay motivated, rather than be put off by the idea that something is too big and insurmountable.

Setting goals gets you into a place of more personal empowerment, a sense of being in control and guiding your life as opposed to sitting back and watching life happen to you. Letting life happen to you is ultimately frustrating and unfulfilling but designing a life that you want and flowing into that life will bring you enormous amounts of personal validation and satisfaction. If, after working through this chapter, you are still confused about what your goals are, keep working through the book and get to know more about who you are. It might take you a couple of goes to work out what you really want in life. Not everyone has this locked in straightaway. Part of the journey of self-discovery and self-knowledge is learning who we really are and what it is we really want after trying out some things that maybe don't fit at that moment.

Or you could ask yourself things like this: if you only had forty-eight hours to live, what would you choose to do? If you only had a year to live, what would you be doing differently over that next twelve months? What kind of conversations would you have? What relationships would you have? Where would you live? How would you choose to spend your time? From your answers to these questions comes your master plan, because that's clearly what you want to be doing.

Feeling stuck

Creating change in any area of life can be a daunting process for some, while for others it's an exciting process to welcome in the new. I've oscillated between both feelings many times in my life. For instance, the thought of moving house fills me with dread when I think about the amount of work it takes to pack up all of my belongings. However, when I think about the new place that I'm moving into, the new, fresh start that it brings, that feeling of excitement and joy is so much more powerful than the grumbling I feel at packing.

At some stage throughout our lives, we have all felt stuck and have not known how to change a situation, whether we were struggling to lose more weight, wanting to be more effective with our time management, wanting to work less hours, have a more fulfilling relationship, or find a more inspiring career. At times, it can feel as though we are standing in the middle of a fog with no way out. Stepping into the unknown can be daunting and create anxiety, especially when we don't know where to start.

We can all feel stuck in our personal journeys from time to time. We can all become susceptible to the nonsense that our shadow selves perpetuate—"you're not good enough", "you'll never get what you want", "who do you think you are?" This feeling of being stuck usually plays out in various ways such as feeling bored in your job, feeling miserable in your relationship, feeling generally unwell and unsettled, maybe even just plain blah. There is a myriad of symptoms, but it all basically presents as malaise and when clients come to me talking about feeling stuck in their lives, it shows up as a message—whatever the delivery system—that tells them they just don't have it all together.

It's vitally important for people to understand that no matter the situation, how tough, raw, painful, or overwhelming in that particular moment, there is a way forward. Life continues despite our moods, feelings, and frustrations, and we have the power to make gentle, kind, and compassionate decisions that will allow us to pivot from our current circumstances. This doesn't mean that we escape the lessons that are being presented to us; it just means that there is a line somewhere and we need to find it. This may mean that we need to look into our spiritual dimension to connect in quiet prayer and listen to our inner voice of wisdom. It might mean that we have to be patient and wait for the solution to become a bit clearer to us. Whatever we need to do in this moment, a solution will come and sometimes that means not taking action but moving around the challenge in a different way.

Throughout my life's stumbles and falls, I've found peace and guidance in the application of all the tools in my coaching toolkit. They have literally been lifesavers to help me quiet my mind and give me guardrails for decision-making when I've felt like my life has become stuck. Using the steps that create change gives me a sense of knowing that I'm walking away from the stuck feeling, and it's just a matter of time before I will be leaving this place of unrest.

The easiest way to formulate a plan to help you move away from feeling stuck is to form a simple plan. This map will guide you toward the actions you can take that will ultimately move you toward where you want to end up. I often refer to the five areas of change that encompass the dimensions of who we are. Our physical self, or Body; our energetic self, or Energy; our intellectual self, or Thoughts; our emotional self, or Feelings; and our spiritual self, or Spirit.

When I feel stuck, or clients come to me and say they're stuck, it's at this point that I begin with a series of questions based on the Five Dimensions of Wellness—body, energy, thoughts, feelings, and spirit.

Let's say you're feeling stuck around your career, and you feel utterly uninspired by what you're doing each day. My approach would be to ask you to take a moment to stop and reflect and work through the five dimensions based on dissatisfaction with your career.

Our bodies

What do you do in your life that increases your endorphins? Do you walk each day? Run? Exercise? Do you feel inspired within your physical body? Do you feel strong? If not, what actions can you take to feel strong and energetic in your body? Doing this increases our endorphins to help us think and feel happier, which connects us to our mind (intellectual self) that promotes healthy thinking and avoids "stinky thinking" or negative thoughts.

Our energy

What thoughts are you having toward your career? For example, do you wake up each morning with dread? Do you look forward to your day? Or do you run late? Do you procrastinate and avoid getting work tasks done? Do these thoughts support you and elevate you, or do they suppress you?

Harnessing positivity in the form of affirmations has a direct impact on our thoughts and whether we're uplifted or suppressed by those thoughts. It is our thoughts that are directly linked to our physical body and energy levels. If you are thinking negative thoughts around work and your career, you will more than likely feel lower in energy than someone who is inspired by what they do. You'll feel disinclined to be at work, to even see the good at any level, in both the activity and, more often than not, the people involved in your work as well.

Conversely, when you are connected to your job through positive thoughts, it feels like fun to go to work. It becomes inspiring and effortless and can even be a joy. That's not to say that every day is going to be perfect, but it's just not the slog that it can be when we are thinking negatively about our work lives.

Our thoughts

What we think, act, and do has a direct impact on how we feel. Our thoughts can drive our emotional state for good or bad. If we think negative thoughts and don't look after our physical body, the state of our emotions goes haywire. We shift out of alignment very quickly and can feel overwhelmed, unable to concentrate, uninspired, and perhaps even depressed.

How can we supercharge and shift our state? Get moving. Move your body. Increase your brain's happiness levels through meditation and positive thinking. Journal. Talk to a coach. Express how you feel. It's when we start to implement some of these actions and kick-start some positivity into our emotional centers that we begin to support all of our dimensions—physical, intellectual, emotional, energetic, and spiritual—and we can then tackle whatever issues are the underlying culprit of any dissatisfaction we are facing.

Our feelings

Our energy system is impacted by our thoughts, our bodies, our emotions, and our soul. When they're misaligned, our energy falters and flatlines. It vibrates at a low frequency and pretty much repels all the positive things that we wish to bring into our lives. When our thoughts, bodies, emotions, and soul are all humming along in unison and we're feeling effortless, our energetic selves are simply brimming with positivity and we generally tend to pull toward us all the things that we have been striving for, and life equates to a sense of wholeness and contentment.

Our spirit

Every one of us has access to God, a higher faith, higher dimension, source, Spirit, whatever you want to refer to "it" as. Accessing this divine wisdom is completely within our power and current abilities. All we have to do is tap into it via prayer or meditation, or whatever form of "quieting practice" is used to get there. When we pray or meditate, we concentrate on lessening the "noise" in our lives and focus on the internal compass that offers us a well of rich guidance. Getting into this quietness and solitude allows us to grow in mindfulness and awareness that creates space, calm, and clarity within ourselves and our lives. We begin to function on a higher level in our routine day-to-day existence. Our bodies, minds, souls, emotions, and the energy of who we are is intrinsically connected, more than we tend to acknowledge; however, it's my deep belief that when all our dimensions work in unison, we thrive and are given the literal space in our lives to create the shift that we desire.

Creating goals

If you want to achieve something in your life, you should write it down. It's as simple as that. If you want to live to your highest potential, then take action along with writing your goal down.

A goal helps you get clear on what changes you want to make in your life, and creates a strategic pathway and building blocks to unlock your true potential. A goal inspires you to achieve more and become more motivated to sustain the focus needed to achieve your goals.

A goal is only powerful when combined with an action plan which bridges the gap between where you are now and where you would like to be. Goals vary from the personal, such as attaining a greater level of personal fulfillment, to professional goals, such as achieving certain business benchmarks, sporting goals, such as attaining a level of competence and achievement, and family goals, which may include leading a more stress-free family life.

I have a favorite saying: "If you don't take control of how you want to live your life, then life will control it for you!"

When we embark upon a process of self-discovery and transformation, we have to spend some time actually working out what we want to discover in ourselves and our lives. So, what goals do you want to set? When creating goals, use the S.M.A.R.T.[1] approach: Specific, Measurable, Achievable, Realistic, Trackable.

---

[1] Doran, G. T. (1981). "There's a S.M.A.R.T. way to write management's goals and objectives." *Management Review*. 70 (11): 35–36

Specific

A specific goal has a much greater chance of being accomplished than a general goal.

Example: An incomplete, unclear goal might be: Get a job. A complete, specific goal might be: To have a new career working alongside inspiring people, where I can develop new skills in my passion for design, earning a minimum of $150,000 per year by the end of August next year.

Measurable

Establish concrete criteria for measuring progress toward the attainment of each goal you set. When you measure your progress, you stay on track, reach your target dates, and experience the exhilaration of achievement that spurs you on to continue the effort required to reach your goal.

Example: To get a new job within two months.

Attainable

When you identify goals that are most important to you, you begin to figure out ways you can make them come true. You develop the attitudes, abilities, skills, and financial capacity to reach them. You begin seeing previously overlooked opportunities to bring yourself closer to the achievement of your goals.

Example: To get a job within two months, working in an environment surrounded by inspiring people.

Realistic

To be realistic, a goal must represent an objective toward which you are both willing and able to work. A goal can be both high and realistic; you are the only one who can decide just how high your goal should be. But be sure that every goal represents substantial progress. A high goal is frequently easier to reach than a low one, because a low goal exerts low motivational force. Some of the hardest jobs you ever accomplish actually seem easy, simply because they are a labor of love.

Example: To get a job within two months, working alongside inspiring people where I can develop new skills in my passion for design, earning a minimum of $150,000 per year.

Trackable

A goal should be grounded within a trackable time frame. With no time frame tied to it, there's no sense of urgency. If you want to lose ten pounds, when do you want to lose it by? "Someday" won't work. But if you anchor it within a time frame—by May 1—then you've set your unconscious mind into motion to begin working on the goal.

"T" can also stand for tangible. A goal is tangible when you can experience it with one of the senses—that is, taste, touch, smell, sight, or hearing. When your goal is tangible, you have a better chance of achieving it.

Example: To attract a job within two months, working alongside inspiring people where I can develop new skills in my passion for design, earning a minimum of $150,000 per year by the end of August this year.

Then we complete an action plan supporting your goal, helping you get clearer on what action you need to take to be successful in achieving your intention.

Your action plan may look like this:

1. Have my résumé up to date.
2. Send my résumé to ten companies I want to work with that inspire me.
3. Ask clients, colleagues, or friends if they know of anyone hiring and follow up these leads.
4. Tell myself each day when I wake up: My dream job is already here!
5. Review my goal each day and visualize myself working in my new space.

Reaching your goals

By definition, one of the key features of any goal is that the goal be attainable. That is, a goal has to be realistic. Another aspect of any goal is that you should consider breaking it down into several smaller goals. When I first tackled the goal of writing a book, I found the idea of writing 75,000 words daunting! So, I looked at it from a different perspective and identified the first step as a list of the subject headings. This method of looking at the issue didn't overwhelm me because I could approach it all in bite-size pieces. I was then on my way to categorizing the next group of activities in the book to a series of key tasks.

These action-focused intentions will help you to not feel as though your overall goal is insurmountable. You'll feel motivated as you carefully journey through your key tasks, one by one, and see them gradually add up to the fulfillment of your steps, and then your main goal, in due course and at exactly the right time for you.

What's the concept behind identifying the steps and the key tasks that combine to fulfill a goal?

- The key tasks are the jigsaw puzzle pieces that you can use to create the steps that will become your ultimate goal, so get moving and note down your key tasks and start completing several of them today.
- As you cross your key tasks off your daily (or weekly) to-do list, you will feel the urge to do more. As they say, nothing succeeds like success.
- The more you get used to seeing yourself being successful, the more you'll want to do.

The effects are exponential. Clearly, the process of seeing your ultimate goal as a series of achievable, smaller steps and key tasks is your secret weapon toward attaining each of your life goals.

Be in the habit of making lists of your goals and then be diligent about listing the steps and then the key tasks en route to the final destination of each goal and you will see real progress each day.

My tip

When you start thinking about creating goals, keep asking yourself these questions:

1. Does this feel right for me?
2. Is this what I want?
3. Does this goal excite me?

4. Am I prepared to do what is necessary to achieve this goal?
5. Have I followed the S.M.A.R.T. process?

Even though you may only set goals once a year, when you do create those goals, I encourage you to think big! Think outside the square and challenge yourself to dream big and create the largest goals possible. If you don't dream, nothing happens!

Task 1: Creating goals

This is your time now to create powerful goals in your new life. Let's take a look at the six main areas where most clients often want to create some level of change.

- Home
- Health
- Financial
- Career
- Relationships and family
- Spiritual/purpose.

Hello Coach!

The diagram above highlights all the key areas in your life that are of high importance. Each circle represents a specific area in your life that you are wanting to change. If there is a specific area that does not appear above, make up your own goal in relation to this area. You may find that sometimes the areas you want to change overlap like the circles above. But try not to have more than ten goals; otherwise, it can become overwhelming.

Keep them short, concise, measurable, and realistic, with a time frame.

There are three steps to this challenge:

The first step is to get clear on what you want. Which area in your life needs your attention but has been neglected for a whole lot of reasons (and excuses)? Spend time on this exercise and really think about where you want to be in three months' time, six months' time, and a year.

The second step is to create an action plan for each of these goals that will help transform this area of your life. An action plan sets out the building blocks and defines the pathway to help you achieve your goal(s). It's one thing to have a goal written down and to read it every day; however, that alone will not help you reach your milestone. You need to take action as well as having the intention or goal. You need a strategy that is simple to follow yet still a powerful prompt or motivator to help you toward success.

The third step is to read and review your goals every day, with passion. A good habit is to check in with yourself and ask yourself honestly how well you are doing in this area. When you are honest with yourself, you have the opportunity to change and be successful in your chosen goal.

In achieving your goals, if you find that there actually is any kind of block somewhere and you are not progressing as well as you want to (plus if you are in denial about your lack of progress), you have reached what I refer to as your roadblocks.

We want to bust your personal self-sabotage roadblocks, because these patterns of thinking and behaving hold you back from reaching your goals. You may need to spend a bit of time here purposefully working through what your roadblocks are and how you are going to move past them. In a lot of cases, the biggest roadblocks that I tend to encounter are easily overcome because it's just a case of you being your harshest critic rather than your greatest champion.

Here are some examples of goals in case you're not sure where to start:

My health goal:

1. To lose ten pounds by April. I will feel fantastic with my new fit body!

My action plan:

1. Commit to exercise with a friend and exercise together three times a week.
2. Eat less starchy foods.
3. Drink more water and think more positive thoughts about my body.
4. Find a picture of a body that inspires me and look at this each day.
5. Identify potential blocks to achieving my goal, e.g. negative thoughts that may sabotage my success. For example, "Why bother? I may as well give up. I will never lose weight. It's too hard to lose weight. I never achieve anything" and so on.
6. Choose to fill my mind with positive messages about my body.
7. Track my progress.
8. Celebrate my success, e.g. reward myself each week I am successful in committing to my action plan by having dinner with a friend, seeing a movie, or having a massage.

The first step

My health goal: _____

My financial goal: _____

My career goal: _____

My relationship goal: _____

My home life/hobbies goal: _____

My spiritual/highest purpose goal: _____

Other area of my life goal: _____

The second step

Health action plan

My action plan to help me achieve my health goal is:

1. _____

2. _____

3. _____

4. _____

Financial action plan

My action plan to help me achieve my financial goal is:

1. _____

2. _____

3. _____

4. _____

Career action plan

My action plan to help me achieve my career goal is:

1. _____

2. _____

3. _____

4. _____

Relationship action plan

My action plan to help me achieve my relationship goal is:

1. _____

2. _____

3. _____

4. _____

Home life/hobbies action plan

My action plan to help me achieve my home life/hobbies goal is:

1. _____

2. _____

3. _____

4. _____

Spiritual/purpose action plan

My action plan to help me achieve my spiritual/purpose goal is:

1. _____

2. _____

3. _____

4. _____

Other area of my life action plan

My action plan to help me achieve my goals in other areas of my life is:

1. _____

2. _____

3. _____

4. _____

The third step

Print or write out your goals and read them each day.

Your affirmation for setting your goals

"I'm attracting new opportunities each and every day."

Daily must-do

Keep up the great work with the "mind chatter" dump. The clarity and peace that this exercise brings is creating that positive space that allows in all the good stuff.

Your review

1. What were my personal highlights during this goal setting phase?
2. What challenges did I face and how did I handle them?
3. What exciting new insights did I discover about myself?
4. What was my greatest achievement in this phase?
5. What is my commitment for the next phase?

Remember

By the end of this book, you will discover what inspires you and who you want to be—and then you'll achieve it.

Your checklist

A. Complete Task 1: Creating goals.
B. Write out affirmation and verbalize daily.
C. Your daily task: "mind chatter" dump.
D. Complete review.

THE POWER OF BELIEF

If you don't believe that change is possible, change will never be possible. No matter what dark points you've had in your life, never underestimate the power of belief in yourself as to what you're capable of overcoming. There will be times when you look at those goals on a piece of paper and have serious doubts as to how you're ever going to achieve them. Wallowing in self-pity and self-doubt is actually a form of sabotage opposed to the force of believing. When you have belief, what you can create is endless.

One thing that I had to learn about the power of belief is that just because I believe in something, it doesn't mean that it's going to happen instantaneously. When I was in my early twenties, I had a deep belief that one day I would be instrumental in positively impacting many lives around the world through my vision of seeing everyone have access to tools to help give them the confidence to create change in their lives, and impact millions of people. I didn't know how I would achieve this. I just believed I would. Day by day, year by year, I never lost sight of this belief even when things appeared to be the opposite. My faith has been a huge strength in my life.

When I started working with the Power of Belief, I found myself frustrated and starting to think that I'd failed some sort of arbitrary test—that my beliefs simply weren't strong enough and therefore my goals weren't being realized. What I had actually failed to see was the connection between my belief and the patience that I needed to have to see my belief become a reality. I originally had made the mistake of thinking that if I believed something and it didn't happen when I wanted it to happen, that meant I was a failure. In fact, the opposite was, and is, true.

You have to hold on to that faith and that belief, no matter what. It's not something you negotiate on a daily basis; it's something you just make a commitment to. If I'm being really honest, the actual ability to be one hundred percent solid in that belief is a work in progress. Overcoming self-doubt and self-criticism is difficult for most people; however, committing to becoming better at this daily practice will strengthen your abilities and resolve. It's like building muscle. You can't just will muscles to happen; you have to diligently and daily build them up and once you're there, you know how to maintain those muscles. It's not difficult but it does require a bit of discipline and dedication.

The nature of belief

Ever since I was a little girl, I've always had a feeling that I would write a book one day. Would you call this believing? I would! There was something inside me that gave me a feeling of certainty.

Over the years, as I busied myself with my career and raised my son, I never stopped believing in my dream. Even though I didn't know exactly how the book would turn out, I never stopped believing in my dream. To believe is to trust yourself. To trust yourself is to believe in yourself and your dreams.

Even though I experienced many setbacks over the years in relation to this dream (and, well, as you now know, they are never really setbacks—there are always lessons to be learned in every situation),

I always held the vision of my dream, believing that, no matter what, it would happen one day.

Originally, I wanted to write and publish this book when I was in my late thirties. I was really driven by the idea of it. I knew deep down that I wanted to reach millions of people with my tools and techniques and in those days writing a book was the way to go—YouTube and the internet weren't what they are today! But it didn't happen. Life got in the way as it invariably does and I just couldn't quite shake the feeling that it wasn't coming together the way it needed to. So, rather than walk away from my goal, I looked at it objectively and accepted that the divine timing of it all meant that there was some lesson for me to learn in the delay that had caused me to pause with the writing.

Turns out that the people I really needed to help me with it weren't available at the time that I was, and I just had to wait it out and learn more about coaching, myself, and life in general. What I can say, with my hand on my heart, is that the delay in getting the book written created the space and availability for the book to be so much better! I'm wiser, stronger, and more knowledgeable, and this book reflects that growth.

When we hold a belief, and we hold it so strongly that no one can tell us otherwise, we send off an energy frequency from our bodies that attracts the opportunities that are in alignment with those beliefs. I believed that I would always have many published books and TV shows, so was it me who created those opportunities or did The Universe pick up on my thoughts and magically open those doors? The answer is that it's both. In order to manifest your desires, you have to have belief that it's possible. There must be no doubt, just a hundred percent pure belief.

The Manifestation Tool—which you'll discover soon—is an example of taking the steps to bring about what you desire, and an important ingredient is having that belief in the first place.

When we're talking about beliefs, we're also to a degree talking about energy. That's the feeling that we pick up on when we walk into a room that feels "charged," or we meet someone that we "vibe with," despite not really saying much at all. If our thoughts are not in full alignment with our beliefs, we're most likely going to be sending out energy or vibrations that indicate that we really don't believe in what we're trying to do, and we simply will perform at a lesser capacity and attract less than optimum opportunities.

If we truly feel that we have an energy block, or our internal vibrations are really out of alignment, we need to work through the Five Dimensions of Wellness and see where we have an issue and address it. In terms of energy healing, we can easily seek out people who specialize in energy clearing—from Reiki healers to shamanic healers, from therapists to neurolinguistic programmers—whoever works for you and your issue, seek these people out and follow their guidance.

The main point here is that you can't think your way through change; you actually have to identify where the issues are and clean up whatever mess or clutter is in the way of living your life's purpose. I'm now living proof of my belief that I would write a book that would give people transformation tools that they could use to discover the power of self-love in order to create change. It has been

my belief that one day I would achieve this goal. And I have …
some thirty years later!

Your beliefs and the art of believing

You might be someone with a number of values (aka "beliefs") but how willing are you to learn the art of believing? Our beliefs and values are usually aligned with our moral codes and our sense of propriety but the art of believing that we can manifest what we truly desire in life is quite a different thing. How many of us can honestly say that we have found it easy to truly believe in ourselves and our goals?

Honestly, I would say that learning to believe in your true potential is an art, and it can be learned. It's a skill you can acquire and develop with daily practice, along with transformational tools I'm going to share with you. On a personal, vibrational level, the beliefs you hold within you about life, reality, existence, money, love, relationships, your self-worth, your abundance options, your friendships, your self-actualization processes, and so on inform your every move.

We are guided by what we feel we deserve and our beliefs about ourselves are constantly writing the script for our lives.

Right now, on a scale of one to ten, how in control of your belief system are you? How much have you deconstructed the beliefs you may have received from others during childhood and how willing have you been in life to develop and create your own version of those beliefs after carefully examining them on a conscious level?

One of the simpler examples of our beliefs is taking a look at what we've dragged along behind us from childhood. For instance, you may have been told by your parents that you needed to earn a lot of money to look after them doing a high-paying job, such as a doctor or a lawyer. You did this, but at the cost of your own joy and satisfaction. This would have been found in being a chef, which potentially could have earned you even more money and recognition along with great personal satisfaction and a connectedness to your true life's purpose. You sacrificed your own beliefs about yourself to subscribe to the view of others, in this case, your parents.

Certainly, some traditional beliefs are well worth keeping; however, there may be others which you might find are actually fear-based and/or limiting. Your ability to believe that certain options are possible for you in life is based on whether or not you are able to hold positive beliefs and values about your own potential. Have you noticed how often people will speak in a way which actually reveals just how unfortunately limited their internal belief systems have become?

I've mentioned before that I have definitely struggled with believing that I was good enough and I have certainly been guilty of using very limiting language around those beliefs, but I have found that as I have concentrated on actively putting a stop to speaking negatively about my capabilities, more opportunities have arrived at my doorstep to encourage me to believe that I actually am good enough. Indeed, if you could know for certain just how dramatically your whole life could actually turn around simply by your being willing to have a suspension of disbelief, you would be astounded. Learning to trust and believe that you are worthy of the best that life has to offer can be a truly life-altering experience.

Here's just a simple example. Many years ago, I needed to move houses and at the time I was really fixed on wanting a white house. Rather than think about how difficult it was going to be, I focused on noticing all the white houses that I drove past on my way to and from work and running errands. I believed that the right one would come along at just the right time. It did, and I was very happy in that little white house for many years.

Would it scare you or excite you if I asked you whether you are willing to believe that all the deepest desires of your heart, including those you dare not up until now reveal or name (even to yourself), are actually possible to manifest, providing you simply believe?

We all know the old saying, "seeing is believing"; however, leading transformational coaches (such as the late Dr. Wayne Dyer) have pointed out that actually you'll see the things you want when you truly believe that they are possible.

Dyer is known for saying, "You'll see it when you believe it" and to this day, his book by the same title is one of his bestsellers of all time. The upshot of this concept is basically that when you embrace and truly resonate with the power of your beliefs, obstacles will be mysteriously moved out of your way and you will be able to move forward with your intentions, provided that they are based on positive, win-win outcomes for all. You'll notice conversely that when someone's beliefs are more self-serving than anything else, The Universe has an uncanny way of either ultimately and/or immediately blocking their paths.

Put simply, if you are not willing to at least try or learn to believe that you are actually worthy of all the goodness and joy in the world, then I'm sorry but there is actually no way that your ultimate goals can be fulfilled. Learning to let go of fear and to absolutely believe that all of your highest ideals and goals are going to unfold for you at the right time is crucial to your experience of attaining each goal.

Believing requires a complete trust that everything will work out. Believing means that you can dare to trust that the powers of love and light, plus peace and power, will constantly be on hand to help you to, firstly, believe, and, secondly, take action to set the ball rolling.

Show The Universe you are ready by taking a deep breath, and by daring to believe that indeed, we are all held in love, all the time.

Trust the process of goodness and kindness in your life and take the time to try to see exactly where that warm feeling inside your heart right now takes you, as you believe in the power of manifesting all that you need and desire, one step at a time.

Task 1: Learning to believe

So, how do we get to that level? First of all, you have to take small steps. Set small goals—even for things that you know will happen—and then trust and let go. See what happens.

You could do this while you're driving. Trust that you'll get to work on time and have an easy commute. See what happens after a week of doing this. If you misplace your keys, tell yourself that you know where they are and then trust that you'll find them at the right time.

Let go. Do something else for a while and see what happens. If you're not sure about a decision you have to make, think of all the possibilities, then tell yourself that you're making the right decision and let go. Forget about making the decision, just for a short period of time. After a while, you'll naturally think about it again—and you'll make a decision easily.

The key is to trust and let go. Sometimes you have to distract yourself so you don't worry. Worry is the opposite of trusting and believing—it's tantamount to saying that you don't believe and that's why you have to worry, because by worrying you can make it better … except you can't. So, get busy—distract yourself and see what happens.

I suggest you start small so that you learn to develop this practice. Then, when the big decisions need to be made, you'll know that the process works and you won't worry. You'll believe that you can, and will, do what you need to do and achieve your goals.

This process is so simple yet so powerful, but it takes time to develop the habit. I've been doing it and teaching it for years, yet sometimes I slip up and have to remind myself of this basic fundamental process.

This practice of believing is vital to your success—without it, everything else you do will be pointless.

Task 2: Create new possibilities

Set aside about fifteen minutes every day for a week. Sit down with a notebook and a pen or at your computer and, as rapidly as you can without stopping to think about what you are writing, write down five to ten endings for each of the following incomplete sentences. Remember to write as quickly as possible, without stopping to think about what you are writing and without evaluating the answers in any way.

1. If someone had told me my needs and wants were important …
2. If I were willing to ask for what I want …
3. When I ignore my deepest desires …
4. If I were five percent more assertive in stating my desires …
5. If I deny and disown my needs and wants …
6. If I am willing to listen to my deepest yearnings and desires …
7. If I were more accepting of my needs and wants …
8. If I were willing to act on my preferences …
9. If I believed I could really have what I want …
10. One of the things I need to ask for is …

Task 3: What actions will you take?

At the end of the week, reread all that you have written during the week and then write five to ten endings for this sentence:

If any of what I have been writing is true, it might be helpful if I …

Your affirmation for believing

"I believe in the power of The Universe as it always provides for me abundantly."

Your daily must-do

At this stage of your process of change, have you noticed anything in your "mind chatter" dump? Has it changed from being somewhat negative to a lot less negative or maybe even positive? Take note of that and congratulate yourself on doing well. Now, keep going. You're really starting to understand how taking time each day to rid your mind of the negative chatter is, step-by-step, creating space for positivity to flow in.

Your review

1. What were my personal highlights during this goal setting phase?
2. What challenges did I face and how did I handle them?
3. What exciting new insights did I discover about myself?
4. What was my greatest achievement in this phase?
5. What is my commitment for the next phase?

Remember

By the end of this book, you will discover what inspires you and who you want to be—and then you'll achieve it.

Your checklist

A. Complete Task 1: Learning to believe.
B. Complete Task 2: Create new possibilities.
C. Complete Task 3: What actions will you take?
D. Write out affirmation and verbalize daily.
E. Your daily task: "mind chatter" dump.
F. Complete review.

VALUES

Values are deeply held beliefs about what is good, right, and appropriate. They are deep-seated and remain constant over time. We accumulate our values from childhood based on teachings and observations of our parents, teachers, religious leaders, and other influential and powerful people.

Values are powerful motivating factors in our lives. People who act in accordance with their values are more likely to achieve their goals. If you want to create real change in your life, you must take time to identify the values and needs that are important to you.

The hierarchy of values

Order and power occur within the values you rate as being most important; chaos and powerlessness occur within your lower values. Each and every person is responsible for his or her own life and the values they set accordingly.

To attain a great level of fulfillment in your life is to know what your values are and live according to those values in these main areas:

- Home (social)
- Health (physical)
- Wealth (financial)
- Career (vocational)
- Love (familial)
- Spirituality (purpose).

Your personal code of values is a statement of what's important to you—not things you want or would like to have, but the elements you literally need in your life to be happy. A value is a principle or quality intrinsically valuable or desirable to you. Values are personal. They are your convictions, your beliefs, and your ethics all rolled into one. Your personal code of values may be identical to your family's values, or they may be dramatically different. What is essential is that these values are imperative to your very existence.

When you aren't clear on your personal values and needs in life, you often find you don't reach your goals. Unless you are clearly defined in this area of your life, you will find yourself in environments and situations that don't support your values. You'll feel unbalanced, uncomfortable, and unfulfilled on a very deep level and you'll find it difficult to reconcile the issues that you keep confronting.

The most important value to me is honesty with oneself. It is the value that I cherish above anything else in my life. The art of being brutally honest with myself about who I am, what I desire, and what is afflicting me has taken me a lifetime to perfect and I'm not a hundred percent there yet—there's always room for improvement—but because of the importance rigorous honesty plays in my life, I spend a lot of time trying to get it right.

When we are not honest with ourselves, we pay ourselves the greatest disrespect and disservice imaginable. We literally take ourselves hostage to illusion and willfully stop ourselves from gaining greater understanding about who we are and what we can become. To add to our disenfranchisement, the lessons that we're supposed to be learning just keep on coming up, again, and again, and again.

If we find ourselves in this dark place, it's imperative that we stop and ask ourselves if we are being honest with ourselves. By answering truthfully, we allow ourselves the freedom to move forward.

The value that I place the next greatest importance on is authenticity. For me, there is true grace and power in owning who we are—our feelings, thoughts, beliefs, gifts, imperfections, all of it. Being present and mindful not only demonstrates a level of self-awareness but also allows us to explore and discover who we really are and what makes us, us.

We are constantly bombarded by messages from mainstream media, social media, celebrities, neighbors, friends, family, politicians, you name it, about who we should be and how we should think, feel, act, what we should wear, etc., and so the space in our minds where we need to critically think can be filled with a lot of "noise" instead of quiet, reflective space that allows us to get to the core of who we really are. When I feel overloaded by the outside world's messages, I turn it all off for a while and look inward. That's when I reconnect with my authentic self and feel strong enough to take on the world anew.

The third most important value on my personal list is health. Having moved through many stressful periods that have placed inordinate amounts of pressure on my health—being a single mom with a young child, running a full-time business, and trying to heal a life-threatening autoimmune illness—I quickly learned how to "get real" about my health and not take it for granted. I feel grateful for having had the opportunity to experience it all and to understand the layers that go into making a person healthy. For me it was not just physical, but energetic, mental, emotional, and spiritual. Once

I figured that out and got all of these dimensions working together, I truly did feel healed.

Whatever your values are, take time in determining what these are for you. Don't be swayed by outside influences. To be authentic in your own life, you need to know what is important to you and make sure you are on the path to having these values met in your life and understand how you can meet them. Honesty is a big part of this process in understanding yourself, what you value, and how to have a life that represents you.

Living your values

Living in agreement with your values is fulfilling; living in conflict with your values is stressful and dissatisfying. That's why it is so important to clearly understand your own personal code of values. Your happiness depends upon not just knowing your values but living in accordance with them. Stress does not result from hard work, long hours, or multiple roles in life. Stress results from conflicts surrounding your values. When put in a situation where you are unable to honor your core values, you will feel stressed out. No amount of relaxation, meditation, or exercise will eliminate the stress until the values conflict is resolved.

A lot of people seesaw between living within their so-called comfort zone or just managing to scrape by, attempting to fulfill their needs and wants by subsisting in either very challenging circumstances (e.g. never having enough), or just cruising and feeling just okay. These situations serve to highlight the experiences of frustration and desperation, not inspiration. They exist in a zone where they do not love who they are, what they do, or in fact much in general.

They are most certainly not seeing inspiration and aspiration guide their lives.

When you live a life according to a design that was written by others, for good or bad, it can only result in disenfranchisement from your core values. For example, suppose you excel at science or math in school because you find it fairly easy. Your parents insist that you go to university to become a doctor (because you're good at science and math) and you'll be able to make a lot of money (your parents have always valued money and job stability over happiness and fulfillment), rather than training to become a chef and opening your own restaurant (being good at science and math are enormously beneficial in a restaurant setting!). You are then living a life that you're not suited to nor honoring your own core values which might be more in tune with job satisfaction and creativity. It's critical that you separate the things that you value most highly from what society, culture, and perhaps even your family values. Ultimately, the only person who is living your life is you and you are not serving the greater good by being miserable and detached from the fundamental ideals that set your heart aflame.

Values are not about right and wrong; as a broad, cultural construct, they are about what's right and wrong for you as an individual, given who you are and what you want in your life. What you truly value is, by definition, right for you. What you value may not be right for those close to you and may be a source of disagreement and dissatisfaction if others attempt to enforce their code of values on you. The level of your values and the hierarchy you determine for these values in your life dictates where you will be in power or overpowered. Any area of your life in which you don't empower yourself, someone else will overpower you.

Values and value

It is important to understand your own personal values because those values are linked to your purpose in life. You might say that your purpose is to live your values. And when you do, life is good; you feel aligned and fulfilled.

Before you explore which values are important to you, start by looking within and value and appreciate everything you do in your life. If you work outside the home as well as run the home, do you acknowledge the amazing role you play in keeping your house clean, cupboards stocked, fridge full, clean sheets on the beds, cooking meals, washing and ironing clothes, running the kids to and from school, picking up your husband from work, kids' sport, ballet, soccer training, driving the older kids to Saturday night parties and picking them up past midnight because you want them home safely? If not, take a moment to reflect right now on how much you are doing in your life and the value that it has.

I remember I had all the "right" ingredients for a new beginning when I ended my first marriage. I thought my new life would naturally feel and look different. It did look different from the outside: new car, new house, new suburb, new career—practically everything was new and fresh on the outside. But what happened to who I was inside? The truth is that very little had changed. There were some key ingredients missing, and all those missing ingredients were solely related to my lack of identification of my values. I didn't have them completely sorted out in my own head or heart and I confess, I struggled for a while.

When we are not valuing ourselves and the things that we do, we often resort to seeking validation from external sources such as husbands, wives, children, colleagues, and friends. We want others to tell us how special we are, how good we are, how well we are doing or coping or overcoming. More often than not, there is a layer of simmering frustration and resentment bubbling away in the background. When others are telling us that we're great, it's nice, but it's really only a superficial Band-Aid®, because we truly aren't supporting ourselves with our own self-determined validation. We are not placing value on any of the things that we do and achieve. We are not recognizing our own self-worth.

When you take responsibility for yourself, for what you think and choose to believe about yourself, and stop looking for external validation and acknowledgment from outside sources, life can really become so much more rewarding, and you may even feel content with yourself and see the value in you! If your world is not reflecting all the constant effort of your work and the hours you put into daily existence, chances are that you are not valuing your role and acknowledging how amazing you really are. When you choose to acknowledge the value you give, you may be amazed at all the compliments you receive back.

When you start appreciating everything you do in creating your day, your world often reflects this value and acknowledgment back to you. Valuing yourself can appear in the way of more loving thoughts and feelings you have about yourself, or a sense of feeling happier and more at peace with who you are. Family and friends may acknowledge you for being a wonderfully caring person, or you may receive a bunch of flowers unexpectedly from a girlfriend who appreciates you. For me, it comes through my son, with his open, loving arms wrapped around me, telling me he loves me. The main point here is that when you value and appreciate yourself, any acknowledgment that comes to you from outside of yourself is appreciated more deeply because you really do trust in the honesty, authenticity, and transparency of it.

Task 1: Creating your list of values

When my world reflects back what I give out, it truly is a magical place to be. Your next task is creating your list of values. How you determine your own personal code of values can take one of two forms. You can:

1. Start with a long list of general values and pick those important to you; or
2. Build your list from scratch based on your life experiences.

The first method, picking values from a list, may subconsciously encourage you to select values you think you should have, rather than those really important to you. The second method, though more difficult initially, will be more accurate and more rewarding. Try both and see which works best for you. There are many values lists on the internet.

To build your own list from personal experiences, follow this process: think of a brief moment when life was especially enriching and ask yourself:

- What was I doing?
- Who was present?
- What qualities or values was I displaying?
- Do I place more importance on society's voice instead of my own?

Task 2: Sorting your values into the core areas of life

After you have decided which values resonate with you, take the list you created and sort the values into the following six core areas of life (example values are given for each):

- Financial: financial independence, knowledge, freedom.
- Spiritual/purpose: wisdom, wonder, purpose.
- Social: accountability, collective responsibility, dignity, education, fairness, humanity, honesty, individual rights.
- Vocational/career: inspire, guide, teach, empower, recognition.
- Health: vigor, vitality, energy, clear thinking.
- Home: peaceful, tranquil, beauty, decluttered space, safety and security.

If your values are not defined by you, the current value system operating in your life will dictate and create your life!

It's important to be honest about your values. If you say that wealth creation is of crucial importance in your life, yet you have no set wealth goals, you spend money, and don't save, you don't have a financial plan, you are not clear on why wealth creation is important to you, you don't value money or have negative money beliefs like "I don't deserve it" or "money is evil", then money is not at the top of your value system and you won't make great wealth.

Financial values

- Do I value money and wealth?
- What actions in my life support this value?

    1. _____
    2. _____
    3. _____

- How am I contributing toward my wealth creation?

    1. _____
    2. _____
    3. _____

Spiritual/purpose values

- Do I have a version of spirit operating in my life, e.g. God, creator, universe?
- What do I do in my life that connects this to me?

    1. _____
    2. _____
    3. _____

Social values

- Do I place more importance on society's voice instead of my own?

- *Where can I start to place more importance on my voice?*

    1. _____
    2. _____
    3. _____

Family/relationship values

- *What values do I live my life by?*

    1. _____
    2. _____
    3. _____

- *What qualities in me do I value?*

    1. _____
    2. _____
    3. _____

- *Where in my life do I allow these values to shine?*

    1. _____
    2. _____
    3. _____

- *Where am I not allowing these values to shine?*

    1. _____
    2. _____
    3. _____

- *What values are important to me?*

    1. _____
    2. _____
    3. _____

Vocational/career values

- *What career values do I have in my life?*

    1. _____
    2. _____
    3. _____

- *What's my purpose?*

    1. _____
    2. _____
    3. _____

- *Am I living my version of this?*

    1. _____

    2. _____

    3. _____

- *Do I wake up each day and love what I do?*

    1. _____

    2. _____

    3. _____

- *How can I become more in alignment with my career values?*

    1. _____

    2. _____

    3. _____

Health values

- *Is having great physical health important to me?*

    1. _____

    2. _____

    3. _____

- *If yes, then how do I take care of my body?*

    1. _____
    2. _____
    3. _____

- *If I don't eat healthy foods, what foods can I start to eat that reflect this value?*

    1. _____
    2. _____
    3. _____

- *Do I want to treat my body like a temple?*

    1. _____
    2. _____
    3. _____

- *If this is important to me, why am I not living this value?*

    1. _____
    2. _____
    3. _____

- *What do I need to start living this value?*

    1. _____
    2. _____
    3. _____

Home values

- *Is having values for my home space important to me?*

    1. _____
    2. _____
    3. _____

- *If yes, what actions can I focus on to improve my home?*

    1. _____
    2. _____
    3. _____

- *If I don't focus on these actions what will the impact be?*

    1. _____
    2. _____
    3. _____

- *How do I show respect for my home space?*

    1. _____
    2. _____
    3. _____

- *Knowing this is important to me, what's holding me back?*

    1. _____
    2. _____
    3. _____

Task 3: Acting on your values

Write down answers to the questions given below. I have included an example at the end of this section to help you if you're not sure what sort of things you're meant to write here.

In what area of my values am I going to begin to create change?

1. _____
2. _____
3. _____
4. _____
5. _____

6. _____

7. _____

What can I do so my values are met more regularly?

(You may not wish to put answers for all of these values if they did not appear in your list above.)

Financial values

1. _____
2. _____
3. _____

Spiritual values

1. _____
2. _____
3. _____

Social values

1. _____
2. _____
3. _____

Relationship values

1. _____

2. _____

3. _____

Vocational values

1. _____

2. _____

3. _____

Health values

1. _____

2. _____

3. _____

Home values

1. _____

2. _____

3. _____

How will I know when my values are being met in each area?

Financial values benchmark

1. _____

2. _____

3. _____

Spiritual values benchmark

1. _____

2. _____

3. _____

Social values benchmark

1. _____

2. _____

3. _____

Relationship values benchmark

1. _____

2. _____

3. _____

Vocational values benchmark

1. _____

2. _____

3. _____

Health values benchmark

1. _____
2. _____
3. _____

Home values benchmark

1. _____
2. _____
3. _____

Example

In what area of my values am I going to create change?

- Financial
- Vocational
- Health

What can I do so I have my values met more regularly?

- Financial: meet with a financial planner regularly.
- Vocational: start a course that inspires me and that I can use in my career.
- Health: have a personal training session each week.

How will I know when my values are being met in each area?

- Financial: I will have savings in the bank!

- Spiritual: I will feel more connected to my spirit and source.
- Social: I listen to my own voice more instead of what society values.
- Relationship: my relationships will be more nourishing and happier.
- Vocational: I will be inspired and passionate in my work again.
- Health: I will have a fitter and healthier body and will fit into my jeans again!

Your affirmation for your values

"I honor my values and needs daily."

Your daily must-do

Every morning, you are going through this process of change. When you're doing the negative "mind chatter" dump, you are creating much-needed space for positivity to flow in as an agent for change.

Your review

1. What were my personal highlights during this intellectual phase?
2. What challenges did I face and how did I handle them?
3. What exciting new insights did I discover about myself?
4. What was my greatest achievement in this phase?
5. What is my commitment for the next phase?

Remember

By the end of this book, you will discover what inspires you and who you want to be—and then you'll achieve it.

Your checklist

- A. Complete Task 1: Creating your list of values.
- B. Complete Task 2: Sorting your values into the core areas of life.
- C. Complete Task 3: Acting on your values.
- D. Write out affirmations and verbalize daily.
- E. Daily must-do: "mind chatter" dump.
- F. Complete review.

AFFIRMATIONS

I love affirmations. If you've ever had a very loud, fearful voice in the back of your head that has been guiding and directing your life for many years, you'll know that it can be downright traumatizing and debilitating. However, if you understand how to recognize the words you need and to bring them into your life on a daily basis, the relief and comfort that you feel by saying a beautiful, flowing mantra is incredibly liberating. Those words of positivity and comfort start to nourish and feed your wise voice that has been shouted down for far too long.

Affirmations have helped me quieten the voice of fear and strengthen my voice of insight and trust. They've helped me to reprogram. I liken it to a process of unlearning all the negative things I had said about myself for many years, and learning a whole new language of love about who and what I am.

For various people, learning to listen and develop that voice of love, nurturing, and positivity can be an overnight process. For others, it will be a lifelong journey, dependent upon those historical stories we've told ourselves.

The power of the affirmation is the "drip feeding" effect of kind, loving words to yourself over and over again that you believe have been missing from your life. Saying, writing, reading these words to yourself make you begin to believe in their truth on a cellular level, and therefore bring them to reality. Powerful affirmations, repeated, begin to reprogram our understanding of ourselves and jolt us into a braver, better recognition of who we are and what we can achieve.

I have long been aware of the power of affirmations in my own life. When I was looking for a new house, I would affirm to myself that I was going to find my beautiful white cottage effortlessly, and within four weeks I did.

When I was setting up my new business my affirmation was "Clients flow effortlessly to me—I've got ten amazing clients waiting for me, ready to go, at the end of my coach training"—and I did. I manifested that, because I believed and because I was filling my brain with really positive stuff that I hadn't experienced a lot of in my own life. I grew up in a very negative environment, as you might have guessed. And I had to work, and continue to work, to overcome that negativity. But I can guarantee that it certainly gets easier and much more enjoyable when you begin to see the fruits of your labor.

However, when I first started practicing affirmations, I felt like a fraud. I felt ridiculous. I'd stand in front of the mirror and say, "You're worthy of love," or "Clients will want to come and work with you."

I felt silly because I was so used to believing the opposite. Then, all of a sudden, I was giving myself all this nourishment and a new way of operating, of being, of thinking, of existing. It felt weird. It felt like trying on a new shirt that I'd taken out of the plastic and hadn't yet washed or ironed and I'd put it on and it was scratchy. It didn't feel right. We need to put those shirts through the wash a few times. And it's the same with us. We need to go through the wash a few times with our affirmations before we really get comfortable with saying and believing them.

For me, it is still a daily commitment and practice of self-belief which centers on using The Manifestation Tool and affirmations to make it all gel. And it feels good.

You, too, will need daily persistence and practice and you'll need to keep coming back to this question: "Are you prepared to do whatever it takes to create change in your life?"

If the answer is no, clearly you're not ready to change and you haven't got tired of your old life. But if the answer is "yes," your affirmations will help you create that change.

The principle of affirmations

Affirmations are simple statements that we make of positive words of reinforcement to help us achieve the change that we want. They may be made on purpose, such as when we want to change some aspect of our life, or they may be made automatically, such as when we tell ourselves, "Oh, this is frightening," when we see a spider in the kitchen. What is fascinating about affirmations is that the more we use them, the more our behavior becomes like them.

The principle behind affirmations is similar to that of drops of water falling on a rock. A few drops will not make any difference to the rock but if the drops fall continuously, over a period of time, the rock will be worn down.

I firmly believe that affirmations, used in conjunction with other tools, are a powerful method to help reprogram our thinking in ways that support our desired change. Affirmations can be used on their own, but you have more chance of obtaining your goals when you use them with other coaching tools.

How affirmations work

We go through our life according to our beliefs. For example, we know, and hence it is our belief, that if we touch anything hot, it will cause burns. Therefore, we don't touch hot things with our bare hands. However, the belief system of small children is not yet formed. They do not know the difference between hot and cold, and are thus likely to touch hot things with their bare hands. If they get burned or, alternatively, if they are told repeatedly that touching hot things is bad, their belief system forms and they will avoid touching hot things. This is a basic example of how affirmations work.

All our beliefs are stored in the subconscious mind. So, if you find that you are unable to make lots of money, or you make money but are unable to hold on to it, it may be due to subconscious beliefs such as "I do not deserve to be prosperous" or "money is bad." In order to change our beliefs, we have to operate at the level of the subconscious mind.

The subconscious mind is like your computer. It takes some input, processes it, and gives an output. It does not think by itself. It does not distinguish between good and bad. If we put garbage in a computer, we get garbage as output. So, in order to change your beliefs and create a new reality, you have to bombard your subconscious mind with thoughts of your desire. While doing so, there are certain dos and don'ts to be followed for optimum use of affirmations.

Use the present tense

Do not use the future tense. If you say, "I will be rich", your wealth will forever be in the future. The subconscious mind tries to literally bring about what it is asked to do. Instead, say, "I am rich" or "I choose to be rich." According to some psychologists, the term "choose" is better as being rich then becomes your choice. Anyway, isn't it true that your present life is the result of the choices you have made in the past?

Be positive

Only positive statements work. It seems the subconscious mind is incapable of dealing in negatives. If you say, "I am not fat," when that statement reaches the subconscious mind, the term "not" is ignored and it becomes "I am fat." So you may understand, it's better to say something in a grammatically positive context, such as "I am slim and fit!" or "I already am at my ideal size!"

Affirmations can be spoken or written down

You can say them aloud or write them down. When speaking, repeat the affirmation emphatically, preferably throughout the day. However, writing is a faster way of impressing your subconscious mind. Do this several times a day.

Repetition

In order to bring about significant changes in your life, affirmations have to be done several times a day until such time that they become a reality. The least you can do is repeat them at least twenty times in the morning just when you get up and twenty times in the evening just before you go to sleep. Write them down at least fifteen times. If you do them for a few days only, the expected results may not come. Be persistent about them; that is, continue doing them until your goals are accomplished.

Self-reflection technique

Stand in front of a mirror, look into your eyes, and repeat the affirmations with gusto. Put energy into saying your affirmations. Looking into your eyes helps to connect deeply with your subconscious mind. However, you have to do this on a regular basis. This is a very powerful technique. I can personally vouch for the efficacy of this technique.

My supercoach tips for using affirmations effectively

- Successful people use affirmations regularly.
- Each day, get clear on your affirmations for the day.
- Put your affirmations somewhere you can read and say them several times a day.
- Be assertive when saying affirmations. The stronger the conviction, the greater the chance of your goal being realized.
- Be patient: it can take months for the use of daily affirmations to take effect in your life.
- Be persistent: repeat your affirmations while looking into a mirror. Do it up to one hundred times per day! You can do it in three or four installments during the day.

Why not take a pocket mirror with you and do it when you use the restroom while you have some privacy? You can always whisper the affirmations quietly to yourself while looking yourself in the eye with love.

At home or any place where you have privacy, feel free to say the affirmations in a loud, warm, and happy voice! Get ready for rapid change. Affirmations tend to work rather quickly once your subconscious mind is on board! Know that the world's most successful people are open about their use of affirmations.

Sample affirmations

I'd like to share some sample affirmations for a few areas of change in your life. Please remember that you may also prepare your own along similar lines. It's a good idea to combine one or more affirmations and, whenever possible, say them in front of a mirror. Remember that you are trying to reprogram a lifetime of thinking habits, and this takes time. If you are repeating the affirmations about a hundred times a day in front of a mirror, allow a period of at least six months to elapse before expecting results. Combining affirmations with creative visualizations can lead to speedy results.

General affirmations for everyday use

1. I am successful, rich, healthy and happy. Things have a way of working out for me.
2. By [your desired date], I choose to earn $_____ monthly by doing whatever ethical, legal work that is necessary. I will do work that satisfies me and is for the greater good of all concerned.
3. I give thanks for all that has been and for all that will be. I deserve the best and I attract the best.

4. I am grateful to life for all that I have received until now and for all that I will be receiving in the future.
5. Everything is happening at exactly the right time and exactly the right place.
6. The past is in the past and that's where it belongs.
7. I can do it.
8. I'm doing it! I'm doing it!
9. Others feel comfortable in my presence and I in theirs. All relationships flow with ease.
10. I feel good about myself and about everybody around me.
11. All is well. Everything that is happening is only for the highest good of me.
12. The past is gone. I live only in the present.
13. I find it easy to forgive.
14. I live with ease, in flow.
15. I embrace change.
16. I'm good at change!
17. Change is fun! I accept and create change when necessary. I'm good at adapting to all kinds of changes!
18. My hard work and commitment create my success.
19. My success is a direct result of my efforts, and my efforts are always successful.
20. I attract successful situations all the time.

Love affirmations

Love takes many forms: the love between a mother and her child, between two friends, between two lovers, between two life partners, or the love you may experience between yourself and your pets. Thus, in one form or another, love must exist in life.

However, just because you want love does not mean that you will receive love. First, you have to give love. Only then will you get love. And in order to give love, you have to first love yourself.

There are different ways of experiencing love. Some people like to be touched and felt; some like to hear love murmurings in their ears; some like love to be demonstrated by gifts. The best way to receive love the way you want is to show it the same way on those whom you love. We attract those people in our life who mirror our own personality. So, if you want people to love you, start by loving yourself, then concentrate on loving others the way in which you wish to be loved.

I've grown to love the power of affirmations over the years. Initially, as you've read, I struggled to use them, but the more I resolved to wrap my mind around them, the greater outcomes I saw when I used them in daily life. I've used many, many simple affirmations such as "I love the feeling of using my light in the world", "I love feeling constantly calm", "I love the feeling of being able to manifest", "I love the feeling of my worthiness", "I love knowing that I have everything I need to be successful", "I love the qualities I have inside of myself", "I love that I can love", "I love that I am loved."

These simple words, all focused on love, have had the powerful action of helping me realign my thoughts when distraction and negative self-talk have seeped into my mind and threatened to derail my plans. One of the key elements that I love about affirmations is their simplicity and immediate effectiveness.

Let the following love affirmations be your constant companion. Create your own if you feel so inclined. Combine two or more and repeat them over and over, preferably in front of a mirror, at least a hundred times daily, for six to seven months. You will find that without consciously realizing it you will become a more loving person and attract more and more loving people into your life.

1. I love myself unconditionally, and everyone else.
2. I am a loving, forgiving, gentle, and kind person.
3. I love myself all the time, no matter what.
4. It's easy for me to love myself.
5. I'm loving and full of love.
6. My relationships are all based on mutual respect and love.
7. I attract and keep love in my life. People enjoy loving me and I feel good about love.
8. Love is good to me, and I trust love in my life.
9. Love is flowing to me and from me effortlessly and at all times.

Prosperity affirmations

We know that money is another form of energy and yet, in my experience, a lot of people tend to have beliefs around money that have been formed and cemented by their past, their parents' past and even their grandparents' past. The relationships that people have around money and prosperity can be the hardest to budge, so don't feel bad if these mindsets take an extra long time to shift.

What is your attitude to money in your life? Do you assert and acknowledge that you deserve abundance in all its forms, including financially? Do you believe implicitly and without reserve that you are worthy of receiving as much money as you desire with ease and grace? If not, why not try reassessing your attitude to money in your life? Along the way, using positive affirmations about money will help you to tune in to a frequency which can't help but see you attracting abundance in the form of money into your daily life!

Here are some useful affirmations to attract money:

1. I always have more than enough money! It's easy for me to attract money.
2. I love money and money loves me!
3. Money is stable in my life. I enjoy planning how to use my money responsibly and easily.
4. I save money every month and I always keep track of my daily and weekly spending.
5. Money is a positive energy in my life. I attract money all the time and I am good at saving.
6. Money has a way of falling easily into my life.
7. Money is my friend!
8. I spend carefully and I allow myself occasional treats because I am steady and sure about money.
9. Money is an easy and fun part of life.
10. I love saving and I feel good about superannuation, tax, and retirement saving and planning.

Forgiveness affirmations

When you choose to forgive others, you are creating a win-win scenario not only for them but also for yourself. Even if you don't condone the action conducted by another person, forgiving them actually sets you free from being entangled in the dynamic.

Learning to remove yourself from what Deepak Chopra calls "toxic situations" is key to controlling your life. However, if you have a friend, partner, family member, or colleague who has inadvertently or occasionally slipped up and hurt you, what you can do is consider forgiving them. It's up to you entirely if you feel comfortable with doing so.

If you would like to try it out, here are some affirmations to get you started:

1. I choose to let go and forgive bad behaviors from others, while continuing to protect myself from harm.
2. By forgiving others, I am free.
3. I can forgive a person, but I don't have to agree with their behaviors.
4. Forgiveness means that I don't allow others to pull me down at all, ever.
5. I allow karma to take care of revenge. I have no need to hold on to bitterness. Justice is served by higher powers. I have no need to hold on to anger anymore.
6. When I forgive, I feel light and free.
7. I can forgive easily while still letting others know what my boundaries are.
8. When I choose to forgive, I still retain my power.
9. Forgiving is easy and feels amazing.
10. Even if a loved one has already passed away, I can choose to forgive and move on from any negative past feelings about them.
11. Forgiving others' ignorant behavior is easy for me. I choose to not be offended by those who are not aware of how their actions may affect others.

Health affirmations

Health and weight-loss is a multi-billion-dollar industry but the most powerful "healthful" tool is free of charge: your mind! Most people experience at least some level of weight fluctuation and/or health challenge as they age. What you could accomplish in your twenties and thirties may bear zero resemblance to what you can do in your forties or fifties or sixties. Affirmations are an extremely powerful way to train your subconscious mind to achieve your goals.

If you repeat the following affirmations up to a hundred times per day, I guarantee that you will eventually see progress.

Try these for starters:

1. It's easy for me to control my weight.
2. I eat only when I'm hungry and I stop before I'm full.
3. I'm in control of this healthy experience.
4. Keeping healthy is easy for me.
5. Moving my body each day creates happiness in my heart.
6. My body is perfect, day by day.
7. I control my weight, my strength, and my endurance.
8. My body is in balance all the time.
9. I make healthy choices all day.
10. I can control my appetite and I control my weight with ease.
11. When I'm healthy—mind, body, and soul—I'm in alignment and balance.

Task 1: Positive affirmation

Every day for thirty days, take a piece of paper, write down the positive affirmation on the left and any negative thoughts opposite it on the right. At some point, people usually stop having negative thoughts in relation to the positive affirmation. Make sure you keep going with the exercise until the thirty days are finished.

Your daily must-do

Checking in with you about your "mind chatter" dump!

Your review

1. What were my personal highlights during this affirmation phase?
2. What challenges did I face and how did I handle them?
3. What exciting new insights did I discover about myself?
4. What was my greatest achievement in this phase?
5. What is my commitment for the next phase?

Remember

By the end of this book, you will discover what inspires you and who you want to be—and then you'll achieve it.

Your checklist

A. Choose affirmations and practice them.
B. Complete Task 1: Positive affirmation.
C. Your daily task: "mind chatter" dump.
D. Complete review.

THE MANIFESTATION TOOL

After I had identified my vision and my goals, and practiced affirmations and the power of belief, it took me a few years to realize that there were reasons why I wasn't reaching the goals that I wanted to achieve.

I am a multidimensional being. I'm a spiritual being. I have a powerful mind. I have a physical body. I have emotions and I have energy. I realized I needed to do more than just sit in the corner of a room and chant an affirmation, because I wasn't just a brain sitting on a pillow—and neither are you. You have an amazing energy system. You have a complete emotional system as well as having an intellectual mind. It makes sense to be aware that you have all these dimensions and know how you can nurture all these dimensions to perform for you.

How can you strengthen all the dimensions of who you are to get out of a negative, locked down cycle of behavior? How can you create bridges between all the dimensions of who you are? Yes, you do need affirmations and visualizations, you need to plan goals, but you also need to be incredibly grateful for everything that you have in your life, which was one of the elements missing from my life.

I have learned that The Universe will always give us what we pay attention to. If we spend our time focused on limiting beliefs and negative thoughts—what I refer to with my clients as stinky thinking —The Universe will send us what we're thinking about. But if we use the powerhouse of grateful thinking, or gratitude, we'll attract all the good things that we've been focused on. Gratitude puts us in a thankful and non-judgmental space that opens us up to becoming a magnet for peace, calm, clarity, prosperity, happiness, abundance, and things that bring our hearts joy.

Life will often present us with challenges that give us an opportunity to think either negatively or positively, and sometimes those challenges will be great, but we have the choice to operate from a negative or positive position. That choice gives us the power to align our thoughts to outcomes that will either pin us down in a place of stagnation and resentment or lift us up to a place of joy and abundance.

I got sick of living my life without joy, peace, and calm. The dissatisfaction that I felt was awful and uncomfortable, so much so that I'm scrupulous about practicing gratitude every day in my own life because I don't want to find myself living in discontent again. To me, it's just not worth it. The equation, for me, is simple. The daily practice of gratitude has shown me so much abundance that I simply can't imagine living life any other way. I realized that it was going to be very difficult to create more wealth—and by wealth, I mean richness and depth, not just money—in my life, health, relationships, career, etc. without recognizing and practicing gratitude and gratefulness. Not recognizing the things you have, and being grateful for them, leads us to start focusing on what we don't have and berating ourselves for what things we think we lack. We are effectively not looking closely enough at what we do have and how to improve it.

Once I realized that gratefulness for the things that I had already achieved was the key to accelerating the changes in my life that I desired, I set about designing a mechanism that would bring all those dimensions of my being together with the tools I was already using—and that is the Manifestation Tool.

It's important to realize that it is not your business to work out how The Manifestation Tool is going to work. Don't get caught up in the idea of how your new life is going to look or how it's going to happen, because that's actually up to The Universe (if you believe in The Universe). What you need to do is get out of your way so change can actually happen.

Why goals aren't always achieved

Have you ever wondered why you don't ever reach your goal after years of trying? Many people write down a goal, years pass, and they still hope it will eventuate one day. I find that quite a few trainers and coaches in the personal development and peak performance world instruct others to just decide on a goal and then take massive action toward it. I have attended numerous workshops, home-study programs, and tele-seminars where the trainer instructed us that all we needed were enough compelling reasons to support why we wanted the goal and then to do whatever it took to achieve our outcome. This approach can work, but it tends not to work as effectively, on balance, because there is no alignment of all the parts of our being toward achieving our outcome.

I believe that many people do not reach their goals because of the inner blocks, fears, and doubts that arise the moment we set a goal. These doubts and fears can be known or unknown to us. Alongside that, contrary to popular opinion, motivation is not always enough to propel people toward their desired outcome.

Let's look at some examples of goals:

- I would like to lose ten pounds.
- I will be in a relationship with the man/woman of my dreams.
- I will be working in my dream job as a designer.
- I will consistently and easily gross $150,000 per year.
- I will have the financial freedom to travel the world.

Often, when writing down, thinking about, or saying the goal, we feel a wave of discomfort, even if the desire to attain the goal is strong. Why might that be? It's probably because part of you is associating either the process of what you are going to do or the outcome of that goal with discomfort (this may take the form of believing you're undeserving or inadequate in some way), displeasure (this could look like others' judgment about your success), or pain (you may think that people will be hurt if you achieve this goal). These areas of discomfort, displeasure, or pain may arise from past experiences in attempting to achieve this goal. Maybe a part of you believes that the process of achieving your goal will be a lot of hard work. Perhaps you are anticipating that reaching the goal will negatively affect another part of your life. There can be any number of reasons for the doubts and fears.

But the part of ourselves that is putting forward all the doubts and fears is "protecting" us and pulling all the tricks it knows (procrastination, avoidance, distraction) to stop you from moving forward. While we call these behaviors "self-sabotage," the more accurate term is "self-protection," because you are essentially protecting yourself from feeling and experiencing the discomfort of moving forward.

As I mentioned, sometimes we are not even consciously aware of why the resistance is there, as the doubt and fear can reside in the subconscious mind. This is where I would recommend supporting yourself more and having an external aid to help you shift these subconscious belief patterns. At times, we all may need a little extra support in dealing with deep unconscious blocks that may appear. If you are in need of some external help, be it in the form of psychotherapy, traditional medication, alternative therapies, healing through religious practices, or whatever it is that will give you sustenance and comfort, please seek these remedies out. I have spent many years working with therapists, doctors, and healers in order to support myself when the going got tough. There is nothing to be gained by turning away from help. Some of our greatest gifts come to us through the help of others.

Roadblocks

By now I'm sure you would have written down your goals. You are clear on what you want to improve in your life and the changes you want to make. This is only part of the process in being successful in reaching your goals. Writing them down and having an action plan is powerful in itself; however, if you are still struggling in making progress toward realizing your goals, there must be a roadblock in the way.

"Roadblock" is a term I give to something that is preventing you from living your dream goal and living a life you love. This is where we can help to locate the trouble spot and eliminate it. If you don't spend time in this area, your efforts will be wasted; your behavioral pattern will create further despair and frustration and the sense that you are literally going around in circles.

There is an easier way. In this chapter, we will work with what I call The Manifestation Tool. It is a step-by-step process for you to review all the key areas required for manifesting a goal. If one of these areas is missing or out of alignment, this is where your roadblock can be found. Once you have identified what your roadblock is, you can unblock it!

Using the Manifestation Tool is a great way to understand where your roadblocks might be. Say you're wanting to create a different career path and you're not manifesting it. Using the tool helps you move through the steps to figure out where you're out of alignment—am I taking the right actions that will move me closer to my goal?; are the words that I'm saying supportive of my goal?; am I clear on my vision?; what emotions come up for me around my goal? When you are able to use the Manifestation Tool, you're able to isolate areas of misalignment or fear, see these impediments in their most simple form, and set about correcting course.

One example of a roadblock story that I can give you about myself is confronting my father about his years of abuse. For many years, I just didn't even have the vocabulary to be able to tell my story to myself, let alone anyone else. I believed that I may have been damaged beyond repair. I was also repeating negative patterns with romantic partners because I hadn't yet dealt with this trauma. Eventually, I came to understand that I needed to face reality in order to stop the unfulfilling path that I was on. And that meant confronting my father about his actions, but it also entailed disclosing these events to my mother. Both of these situations were difficult for me to face, but I firmly understood that if I didn't face them, acknowledge them, and move on from the trauma of my past, I would never position myself to be happy. I did finally address the pain, learn from it, and release the hold that it had over me. Regardless of what situation or background story is driving your negative behavior, there is always an opportunity to heal these patterns to help create a life with joy and peace and ultimately freedom to be who you are.

Task 1: Identifying negative thoughts

When thinking of your goal, write down whatever negative thoughts come up. You can close your eyes and picture yourself being, doing, or having the goal. Your goal may be attaining your ideal weight, having a relationship with the person of your dreams, or looking at your bank balance and feeling good about it. Don't stop and edit your thinking; write whatever comes up.

Here are some examples of negative thoughts that can arise. If you catch yourself thinking negative thoughts, simply choose to notice them and every time you breathe out, release them:

- I tried dieting. It's really hard to lose my weight and it didn't work before—what makes me think I can lose the weight now?
- The last two dates I went on were uncomfortable. I don't want to go through that again. I will never find a great relationship.
- No one will want to hire me as a designer as I'm not good enough.

- To make $150,000 each year, I am going to have to work even longer hours. Right now, I'm struggling working the current number of hours I'm doing as it is!

After you have done this exercise, try rewriting these thoughts in a positive mindset, without the negative self-talk taking over. For example:

- Even though I tried dieting and it didn't work before, I'm willing to commit to my routine now. I accept myself and am willing to give it another go.
- Even though the last two dates I went on were uncomfortable and I don't want to go through that again, I accept how I feel about it and am open to a new, positive dating experience.
- Even though I feel frustrated as I don't know how to market myself as a designer, I am open to learning and attracting the right resources to me.
- Even though the thought of earning more money makes me nervous about how I'm going to do it, I'm open to the possibility of this happening effortlessly.

My tips

Reaching a goal successfully is not going to happen unless you reflect on what has worked and what isn't working to achieve your goal. Listen to yourself and the words you are saying to yourself. Are you filling your mind with negative self-talk or fueling it with positive talk?

Change your approach if needed and review the actions you are implementing. Being successful in achieving a goal requires a daily commitment, combined with taking action. Saying positive words and reading your goal each day isn't enough if you are really serious about creating something new in your life. You have to continually ask yourself what you are thinking and feeling and what your self-talk and action are in relation to your desired goal.

Task 2: Use the Manifestation Tool

Use the Manifestation Tool to work on realizing your goals. Here is my eight-step formula:

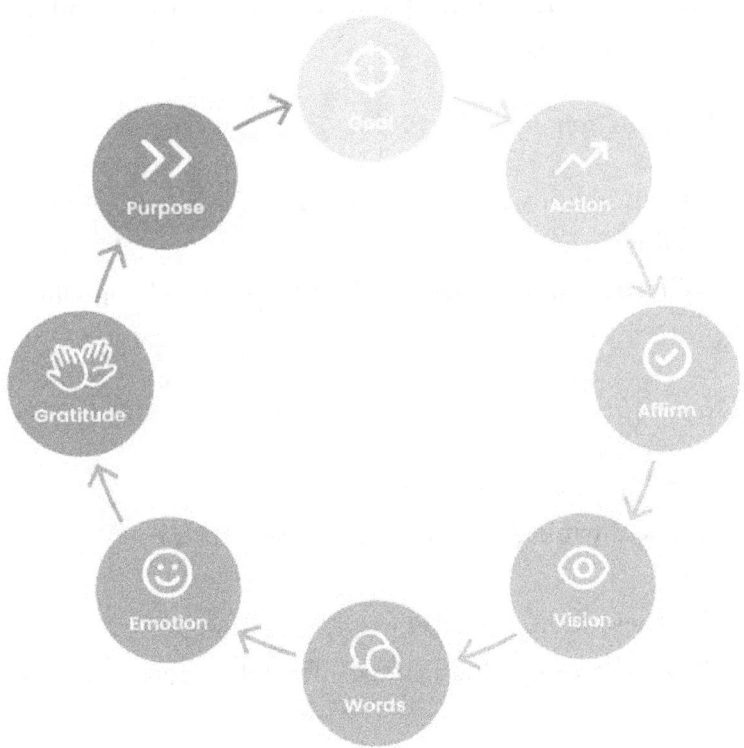

Write down answers to the following in your journal or notebook.

First step: Goal

- What are the goals I desire?
- Am I clear on my goals?
- Do I truly want these goals?
- What five things do I need to change to make my goals real?
- Can I feel it in my body?
- What actions are needed to get in touch with this feeling?
- Do my actions support my thoughts? My vision? My feelings?
- What actions do I need to do differently to be in alignment with my goals?

Second step: Action

- Do my actions support my thoughts? My vision? My feelings?
- What actions do I need to do differently to be in alignment with my goals?

Third step: Affirm

- Am I thinking positive thoughts?
- What affirming words can I choose to think and say each day?
- Do these thoughts support my goals?
- What five things can I think differently about in view of my goals?

Fourth step: Vision

- Do I have a clear vision of my success?
- Do I have pictures that remind me of my success?
- What actions can I do now to create this picture of success?

Fifth step: Words (Manifestations)

- I Believe this is possible
- I am surrounded by Blessings
- I have Clarity on what I want
- I openly receive all the Abundance available to me
- I Change with ease
- I have deep Gratitude for me and my life
- I take Action steps with ease

Sixth step: Emotion

- Can I imagine how it feels to be successful in my goal?
- Can I feel it in my body?
- What actions are needed to get in touch with this feeling?

Seventh step: Gratitude

- What things am I grateful for in my life each day?
- Write down five things each day to remind you to be grateful for everything you have in your life. If you don't appreciate and become grateful for what you have, you will not be happy with more.

Eighth eight: Purpose

- Am I clear on my bigger purpose?

- How will this goal help me in my life?
- How will the benefits impact others around me?

Your affirmation for your manifestation

"I only think positive loving thoughts about myself. I'm loving, lovable, and loved."

Your daily must-do

As you continue to work through your daily "mind chatter" dumping exercise, have you noticed the creation of space for positivity that this practice has created for you? Is the process getting easier? Is it getting harder? Have you rediscovered things about yourself that were long buried? Take note and be grateful. This daily ritual is a small but incredibly effective agent of change and all the little parts build on each other to eventually become something big and spectacular.

Your review

1. What were my personal highlights during this manifestation phase?
2. What challenges did I face and how did I handle them?
3. What exciting new insights did I discover about myself?
4. What was my greatest achievement in this phase?
5. What is my commitment for the next phase?

Remember

By the end of this book, you will discover what inspires you and who you want to be—and then you'll achieve it.

Your checklist

A. Answer the question at the start of this chapter.
B. Complete Task 1: Identifying negative thoughts.
C. Complete Task 2: The Manifestation Tool.
D. Write out affirmation and verbalize daily.
E. Your daily task: "mind chatter" dump.
F. Complete review.

Hello Coach!

YOUR TOOLBOX

The Manifestation Tool is just one of the tools you should use throughout this process of transformation. This chapter contains a list of all the tools available to you. These tools should be used in conjunction with the tasks given to you in each chapter. They will help you shift to the next phase and help you overcome challenges you may face along the journey.

Sometimes your tasks will already use one or more of these tools, but you may wish to use more. There are various suggestions for how often you should use these tools. It's great if you can use them according to the recommendations, but please don't turn them into an added source of stress!

Daily

"Mind chatter" dump

Make the commitment to do the "mind chatter" dump every day, not just on the day you do your tasks. It's a great way to declutter your mind and soul before your day begins and negative thinking has a chance to take over. Give yourself the space to empty thoughts, feelings, and words to clear your day for positive thoughts to come in. You may experience a lot during these daily writings—everything from sadness to happiness. However, as you become more comfortable with this exercise, you'll notice that it has created a space not just for positivity to step in, but also for gratitude, kindness, and clarity to thrive.

Affirmations

Self-talk is powerful: your thoughts create your reality. The more you focus on something, the more chance you have of manifesting your desire. Telling yourself positive thoughts each day reinforces the change you want to take place. Try it out and watch what happens!

Remember earlier in the book when I mentioned that I really struggled with affirmations when I first started doing them? I felt disingenuous and it took me a really long time to get comfortable with them. It's not worth struggling to get on board with these, so why not check out an app or grab a book and kick-start the process. Just reading someone else's writing can feel like the key to unlocking your own ability. It will help you get in the right headspace and before you know it, you'll be writing up, and saying, affirmations that are incredibly powerful and singular to you.

Visualization

The power of visualization is important if you want to gain a strong sense of your dreams and feel them coming to fruition. Spend time each day visualizing your desires and imagine yourself in the scene.

Visualization can be enhanced when combined with the practice of meditation. It doesn't need to be complicated. It can be as simple as spending five minutes in quietness and focusing on a mental image of how you want to be. But feel free to take things up a notch and explore the power of guided meditations that fit with your current state of mind or needs. There are plenty of online resources, from meditation apps to YouTube and even classes (both online and in real life). A small investment in time and researching your best-fit can elevate this practice. And it might just be an easier way into visualization if you're struggling with this concept.

Listening to your intuition

Trust yourself. We all have a voice inside us that is our wise person. It guides us, talks to us, heals us and protects us if we know how to listen to this part of ourselves. Start listening for your inner voice and listen to what it tells you. This voice is the voice of truth and higher guidance.

Don't panic! This one takes a little bit of time to get used to. Not all of us are on the same page about listening to our intuition or, more importantly, trusting ourselves to make the decision that is best for us. But this is something that we can master if we take the time to really pay attention.

However you regard your intuition, whether it's your heart, your inner voice, or your gut, you need to let that voice become stronger. Again, if you think meditation will help you here, use it. It's also worth noting that when you have to make a decision about something, why not practice listening to this inner voice and see what it has to say about things—not just doing the most pragmatic or rational thing. The intuitive and the rational may well align, but if they don't, try mentally exploring the intuitive in case that voice is giving you the best possible answer.

Letting go and trusting the process

This behavior is crucial to completing the program successfully. In order to create change, you need to be able to let go of the past and trust the unknown. There is no magic crystal ball we can ask for advice except to trust in who we are and what feels right for us. Believe in all the hard work you've put in so far. You have diligently been working through all the exercises and completing the steps. If you feel that there is nothing else to do except to "believe," you've arrived at the right destination.

Weekly

Setting and reviewing your goals and intentions

This is one of the most important tools in the Toolbox. If you don't know what you want or where you're going, how do you know when you arrive? Be clear on what you want and put an action plan in place to help yourself get there.

Meditation and connecting with your spirituality

Somewhere along the journey, you will want to find a deeper part of you that has been lurking in the shadows. Finding your version of spirituality or meditation is your individual journey. Even though I may refer to The Universe, The Goddess, and so on, there is no "right" way to experience your spirituality except to trust what is right for you. Ideally, you would meditate as often as possible, but start by making it a weekly practice as needed.

These days, there is a plethora of online guides, apps, and books about meditation. There's also plenty of scientific research to back up the benefits of meditation and mindfulness. I suggest that there is no one-size-fits-all approach to starting out with meditation and continuing the practice, but I will say that it's a practice. Some days are easier than others but showing up is more than half the battle. You just need to spend a bit of time finding out what works for you.

You might also feel more comfortable with traditional religions and that's great too! Whatever form of spirituality speaks to your soul is the right one for you and you'll know it without having to deliberate or second-guess yourself. It'll just be right.

Thought-changing exercises

These are a great tool to be used whenever you feel stuck in a particular thought pattern. Writing out negative beliefs and transforming them into positive, healthy, and uplifting beliefs attracts greater prosperity and positivity in all areas of life.

Here is an example:

First, identify things you would like to change in any area of your life—money, family, relationships, health, hobbies, friends, career, etc. Now write a list of statements about them. The idea is to write down your truth—what you really say to yourself. For example, "No matter what I do, it never seems to be good enough and neither do I."

Second, take responsibility for having chosen those certain beliefs and look very earnestly at where they have served you. You can only let them go once you can clearly see how they have worked in your life, so think about how they have worked for you, honor that for a moment, and now boldly choose to change them. Write the following statement at the end of the list: "I acknowledge that

I chose for [xxx] to occur. However, now I choose to change these thoughts and behaviors."

If your wardrobe is currently filled with clothes that no longer fit, or are completely no longer your taste and you're ready for a new look, wouldn't you clean out your closet to make room for the new gear? Similar to clothes, your mind and soul need decluttering and detoxing so the new desires can come in. Clear out that old stuff that keeps you tethered to the past: this includes limiting beliefs and thoughts, routines, habits, and situations that no longer serve you. You could shed pounds' worth of baggage and feel wonderful!

Body work for deeper unconscious issues

Embrace change. There may be times when you feel that past circumstances keep you locked into a negative cycle of thinking and behaving. It's important that you recognize that you might need some extra help in this area and to seek support accordingly. There are many professionals out there, from trained psychiatrists and psychologists, therapists, and doctors to practitioners of alternative therapies such as kinesiologists, naturopaths, Reiki healers, neurolinguistic programming, masseurs, acupuncturists, etc. The key to unlocking your unconscious blocks is to first, be open to doing so, and second, finding the right person to help you. That person is not going to be the same for everyone, it's not a one-size-fits-all designation, but they will ensure that you are clearer in your way forward.

The Manifestation Tool

This is a must. It is a tried and tested model I developed for myself and my clients. When used powerfully, it creates positive change, attracting new opportunities into your life. You may wish to use the Manifestation Tool on a weekly basis instead of as needed; however, the frequency of use depends on what's best for you.

The Roadblock exercise

As you work through this book, you will keep confronting roadblocks; this is a normal part of the process. Following the exercise will help you move through those roadblocks—you don't want to move around them because they'll still be there! Just further down the road. You really have to dig deep and explore the roadblock so you can stop repeating the behavior in the future. This exercise helps you understand how your thoughts and actions equal your outcomes.

PART III

THE DIMENSIONS OF YOUR LIFE

THE FIVE DIMENSIONS OF PERSONAL WELLNESS

Each human being can be said to exist in five dimensions: physical, energetic, intellectual, emotional, and spiritual. In order to create real change in our lives, we need to change on each of these five interconnected levels.

It's not enough just to change your body or your living space; if you don't change your thoughts, the actual physical changes won't matter.

Similarly, if you change your thought patterns but don't connect to your spirituality and your emotions, you will be disconnected from fundamental parts of who you are.

The five dimensions of our lives are all linked, and no single dimension is more important than another part. They all need to be working in tandem for us to be able to effect the change that we seek. As the saying goes, we are only as strong as our weakest link.

Hence, I created what I call the Five Dimensions of Personal Wellness to incorporate all the five dimensions of human existence: body, energy, thoughts, feelings, and spirit. When we work on all these five aspects to create transformation, we understand completely how multidimensional we really are. When we have our Five Dimensions of Personal Wellness in alignment, we experience a wholeness within ourselves.

The penny dropped for me about the five dimensions when I was sick and on a personal quest to heal myself from the inside out. I was in India beginning a journey of spiritual reawakening. I was seeing for the first time how the physical, intellectual, emotional, energetic, and spiritual were all connected. If one of these five elements was not "well" or "healthy," that misalignment would cause the other elements to be out of balance and the whole system would simply not work as optimally as possible.

I realized that if I didn't work on seeking balance and healing within each individual dimension, I had no chance of achieving overall health and wellbeing when all the elements were brought together. It's like trying to drive a car with a flat tire; it will go but it just won't go very far, and you'll end up damaging a whole lot of other parts of the car if you keep trying to drive it.

I saw for the first time that I couldn't spend time just fixing one part of my whole being—like working on my physical self by spending weeks and weeks in India—without looking at all the parts that made up my whole being, like what negative and limiting thoughts I was holding on to that were impacting my emotions, my energy, my spiritual life. This "aha" moment was so profound for me, and so simple.

I had literally gone to the edge of my own mortality to figure out that I held the key to my own healing. (I'm not suggesting that everyone needs to go through these kinds of extremes to figure things out; this was part of my journey.) I had to include doctors, nutritionists, naturopaths, coaches, etc. but I ultimately had to gain control of who I was and the pillars that made up what I was. My willingness to uncover everything had been keeping me misaligned. Working toward that realignment has become a cornerstone not only to my own life but also to my coaching career which brings me untold amounts of personal joy and happiness when I see clients bring their five dimensions together in unison.

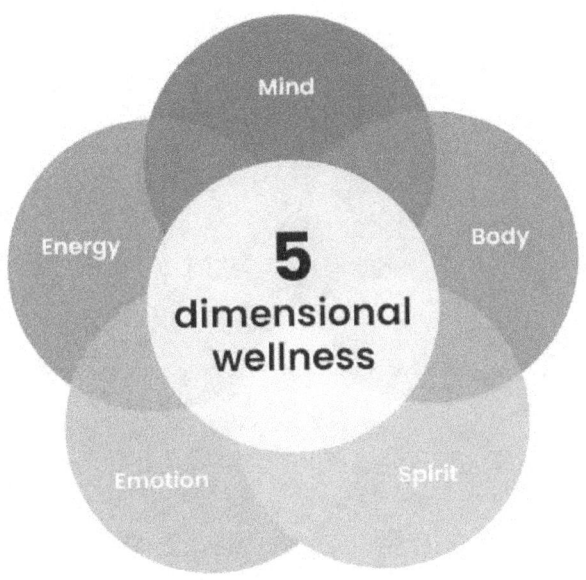

BODY

Addressing the physical side of ourselves requires us to break down the whole into smaller, digestible pieces, from the temple of our bodies to the places that we live and work, the places that we wish to visit either frequently or infrequently, our mindset about how we take care of ourselves physically (from nutrition to exercise, mental health to spiritual health), and everywhere that we tread in the physical realm (our home, car, place of work, place of worship, places we find in nature)—all of it.

I've previously mentioned the life-threatening illness that I faced in my early thirties. It was a scary time for me, but it was also a wake-up call about ignoring what was going on inside my body that I needed to examine and get into balance again.

It's not uncommon for people to overlook the link between their physical world and the chaos in their lives. This connection can be missed because it can be so obvious and mundane. If the link between our physical self, our body, and our home, for example, is weak, it could show up in such ways as having a cluttered home with way too much junk in it, and never being able to find what we're looking for. Another example might be that our unhealthy eating makes us feel like we're thinking through a mind fog. If we don't pay attention to the connections between our physical selves and our surroundings and set them in order, we are falling short of setting ourselves up for maximizing our full potential.

Working on the physical dimension also involves asking yourself: Where am I currently cluttered? Is my body internally cluttered? Do I need to be looking at what I'm actually putting into my body? Is that helping it perform at an optimal level from the space that I work in? Where is it cluttered? Where am I energetically blocking all the new from coming in? How is my inability to manage time related to how I handle change in my life?

You're about to find out the answers to all these questions.

Nourishing the body

I know that I've referred to eating healthily rather indirectly so far in *Hello Coach!*, but I'd like to take a moment here to pause and take a deeper look at nutrition and its importance in terms of taking care of your physical body.

When I was suffering through my illness, I had no idea about how the food and drink that I put into my body directly affected how I felt and thought. Once it was pointed out to me by various doctors, healers, and nutritionists, I began to really pay attention to the connection and the simple equation of what I put into my body equaling what I would get out of it. Simply put, the better quality the gasoline I put in the engine, the better the performance.

For me, it's a matter of maintaining my health and fitness generally, from watching what I eat to exercising and meditating, but I have learned along the way that there are many experts available to help guide me in the direction that is precisely right for me. I recommend that you too spend some time researching what is the best form of fuel for your body.

I have learned that there are certain foods that I'm allergic to and I need to stay away from those. As I've aged, I've also discovered that the ice cream and cake I used to love doesn't agree with my system so much anymore, so I limit the sweets to occasional treats and really relish the pleasure when I do eat them. I've also found an exercise routine that suits my fifty-year-old self, and I go with it. Some days are easier than others, of course, and sometimes I stay in bed under the covers and read too, because rest nourishes my body as much as movement. The key to my body at this point in my life is constantly monitoring and readjusting to what is working and what is not. As I've matured, so has my palate. As I've aged, I've learned how to move my body through exercises that bring a smile to my face and feel good while keeping me healthy. What I was doing in my twenties isn't what I love in my fifties, and so it goes. I just keep asking myself if what I'm doing to my body is helping it maintain its optimal output, and if it's not, I adjust. It's naturally a work in progress, but one that I love because I just feel so great when everything is working in sync.

Creating space and the importance of doing so

Looking at the physical space you live in, operate in, think in, and exist in is absolutely crucial to your process of change. You will come to realize that all the old stuff that you've got piled up, whether it's in your closet, in your office, your garage, and so on, may be adding to a sense of disorganization and lack of clarity.

If your physical space is out of control, consider saying goodbye to anything you don't need. This means letting go of people who no longer serve you, getting rid of clothes, office stuff, and garbage—old stuff that is not only physically cluttering up your space but energetically blocking the new you from coming in. The new you will never come in while you continue hoarding.

For me personally, I need a physical space that gives me plenty of room to think, relax, create, and breathe. I just can't operate in a space that isn't organized and cohesive. Don't get me wrong—I sometimes feel overwhelmed when papers overload my desk and I've got too many books piled up on my nightstand, but I know that paying a little attention to this situation will set me right again once I go through everything and collect my thoughts. It's taken me years to train myself to eliminate clutter and excess. It's become a ritual: when in doubt, throw it out.

Learning to eliminate clutter—finding out what's out of control and eliminating it—will help you to clarify what's not working.

It's a brilliant example of how your external and internal worlds are connected. If you want to create a new you, clearly you need to let go of anything superfluous. That means stripping everything that's unnecessary away, and saying to yourself you are ready to embrace the new and release the old.

While working on this book, the lease on the house that I was living in came due. I'd moved into the home rather abruptly after the end of a very tumultuous five-year relationship. My son and I had found the home to be a sanctuary of healing for us. It was the perfect place for me to mend my broken heart and focus on myself and my son. I surrounded us with all the things that I felt would bring me peace and stability and I really strove to create an environment of tranquility. The lease ended after two years and I realized that it was time to move on. The house had served its purpose—to create a space for healing—but now I needed to create a new space with different energy that I would need while I was launching *Hello Coach!*

I'd like to talk a little about letting go of people who drain you and no longer serve you and are cluttering up your space. As we mature through life, it's no surprise to find that we often outgrow people and situations. Suddenly friends, family, co-workers, acquaintances, and the spaces where we interact with them are completely at odds with who we are internally. It's uncomfortable and we can literally struggle with how to maintain distance from these people or to let them go from our lives entirely.

In life, we generally attract mirrors of ourselves; like attracts like. It therefore follows that if we're in a negative mindset, we're more than likely going to unconsciously be attracting people with similar mindsets to us. However, as we evolve away from negative "stinky thinking" and start focusing on positive, more balanced ways of approaching life, then we're likely to attract more of these types of people into our orbit.

It's awesome when the negative stuff in our life starts falling away because we've started to gravitate toward higher thinking and vibrations. Conversations and conventions that previously took up our time, and caused us stress and worry, shift to reflect who we have become and tend to lift us up instead of bringing us down.

It becomes more difficult when we're faced with circumstances, or people, that are harder to move away from. Perhaps it's family or a work colleague who we need to interact with. This is where boundary setting, such as limiting the time spent with a person, or stating that certain topics of conversation are off the table, can help. It's important to be vigilant about boundaries because they reinforce where you're at physically, emotionally, intellectually, energetically, and spiritually. This approach always works better when doing so with firm kindness.

It's also worth considering taking another look at the situation from a different angle. In most cases, people are always good at something. Focusing on what another person is good at opens you up to concentrating on their better selves and you usually find that the more negative sides of that person tend to lessen in your interactions with them. It's a win-win for both parties.

Ultimately, you always have a choice about where to focus your attention and energy. If people and situations are not serving you, it is well within your capabilities to move away from them. I often say to clients that I can tell more about you by the top five people you spend time with. Certainly a fact worth considering.

Creating space always makes you feel better physically and emotionally. Once you have eliminated the things that have been draining your energy, you can actually feel the energy move back into your body. Most of my clients—and I can attest to this myself—report back after this exercise saying that they just feel lighter!

Your decluttering task

Look around the room you're in. Is there an area where you are sitting that needs your attention? An overflowing wastebasket, perhaps? Old clothes? Piles of papers? If you are like most people, you've probably been meaning to get to that clutter for a while—and the combination of negative self-talk ("I don't have enough time to clean up" or "It's too hard to clear out this clutter") and visual mess drains your energy.

The objective of this exercise is to help you create a plan to declutter your space. This decluttering means not only looking at your physical space but also your emotional, energetic, and mental space—your thoughts.

Task 1: Writing task

Choose a thirty-day period and commit to writing a minimum of three pages of your thoughts every morning, by hand. Hold this time of day as sacred and see it as an opportunity to connect with your inner wisdom or your wise self.

Don't worry about what to say or punctuation, spelling, being smart and creative, or whether you can fill the page. Find a safe place and go for it!

Before you reach the end of this exercise, I believe that you'll have identified some "clutter," or negative self-talk, in your thought patterns and you'll be feeling energized to make the changes required to eliminate this thinking.

Your affirmation for your physical clarity

"Creating space allows me to feel clear and focused."

Your daily must-do

It's time for that "mind chatter" dump. I'm sure that by now you're recognizing the space that negativity takes up in your day-to-day, and I am also sure that you're seeing how this can be overcome by excising it from your daily activities just with the act of writing those thoughts down each day. Keep going—positivity is flowing.

Your review

1. What were my personal highlights during this physical phase?
2. What challenges did I face and how did I handle them?
3. What exciting new insights did I discover about myself?
4. What was my greatest achievement in this phase?
5. What is my commitment for the next phase?

Remember

By the end of this book, you will discover what inspires you and who you want to be—and then you'll achieve it.

Your checklist

A. Complete Task 1: Writing task.
B. Write out affirmation and verbalize daily.
C. Daily must-do: "mind chatter" dump.
D. Complete review.

ENERGY

You have now moved through the physical layer. It may not "feel" like you have experienced change on this level, but the change is happening, and cumulative. As we move into the energetic layer, you will find that there are fewer tasks. The work that you have done thus far was designed so that you'd be free to enjoy the move through the energetic dimension.

We are all energy. Energy isn't something you can see but it's something that you can feel. Most of us understand energy in terms of the natural environment. We understand the energy of the sea and the sun and the trees.

Humans are no different. You can feel when your energy's depleted, you can feel when it's effervescent or high, the same as feeling when it's a windy day or when the sun is strong. You are aware of the feeling or vibe that a house gives off, or that feeling when you walk into a meeting that is charged, either positively or negatively. The most common energy that people can identify and relate to is the feeling you have when you meet someone new and words haven't even been exchanged. Sometimes it's amazing and you feel connected immediately. Other times it's not right and you can feel warning sirens going off in your whole being.

One of the essential things that I do when I work with clients is bringing awareness to the interconnectivity of their conscious and unconscious belief systems and their own body's energy field. It's basically the vibe that you're giving off. It's that energy field that surrounds them at a job interview or on a date; if they've got a business, that's the thing the customers feel when they walk into a shop or office. It's essentially "reading the room"; you can just feel when you're welcome and when you're not.

The energy that we give off in the world, without a doubt, is stronger than the words that come out of our mouths. And it is that tangible, yet invisible energy that most of us have disconnected from. We have, for a variety of reasons, alienated our energetic selves from the rest of us and that lack of connection leaves us unaware of our impact on others. We may find ourselves living completely in our heads and truly incapable of understanding that the energy we're radiating doesn't even come close to representing who we essentially are.

If you find that people are being rude to you in the street for no reason or people are slamming doors in your face, it's probably not that the other person is in a bad mood. It may be that you need to stop and ask yourself, "Who am I being in order to attract this type of energy into my life right now?" What is your energy saying to that person? What are you thinking about yourself in that moment and how is that being integrated into your body and released out to the world?

Your energy dimension starts operating the moment you're born. But over time, you can shut that energy down, like your intuition, through your stories and experiences of life. These become layers upon layers in your energy field and in your energy being that dictates your life. Because energy is more powerful than words, it's almost like you're a magnet. Like attracts like. If you have certain feelings and thoughts sitting in your energy that you are projecting into the world, you're going to attract that back. So not only do your thoughts create your reality but I absolutely believe that the energy that you're carrying or projecting into the world is creating life as you know it.

When I first discovered that I was sick, I knew something was wrong before I was formally diagnosed. I was suffering from headaches and fatigue and I just didn't look as healthy as I knew I should have. I had been working solidly for a number of years, all the while parenting my son, for the most part alone. I was trying to be a superwoman and falling short. My energy wasn't great and I was pushing through, ignoring all the signs. Then the doctor gave me the news that I was headed for life in a wheelchair, if death didn't claim me first. I was stunned! However, I knew instinctively that death wasn't an option, that I would have to find a way to move forward and that would involve changing my energy. I was going to have to lift it out of the slump it was in.

Naturally, finding a way through illness wasn't just about creating more positive energy vibrations, but I placed a lot of emphasis on shifting from a negative space to a more positive and calm space. For me, I deepened my meditation and spiritual practices and investigated ways to increase appropriate nutrition, rest, and exercise into my daily routine. Focusing on these elements really did create a terrific platform for moving my energy toward a happier mindset.

Changing your energy by kidding around

Do you ever feel that life is just one long routine day after another? You wake up, take a shower, have breakfast, brush your teeth, get dressed, go to work, come home, get something for dinner—blah, blah, blah. Well, if you can't face another day of the same old stuff, it's probably time for a "play break."

The idea of scheduling a spontaneity break probably sounds like a contradiction in terms, but when you consider how our society lives and thrives by the clock, it makes sense. Too often, we fall into the trap of believing that life will become easier and more meaningful when we get really good at living and acting efficiently. But schedules, clocks, and well-planned time can quash your creative spirit—the part of you that thrives on spontaneous, open-ended time.

I love open-ended time. In other words, I love to have an afternoon or day to myself to do what I want without needing to be anywhere at any given time. As a matter of fact, I can become pretty tough to live with when my calendar gets too full of scheduled appointments—just ask my family!

When I have open-ended time, I often stop, close my eyes, and check in with myself to determine what feels right in the moment. Sometimes when I check in, I get a goofy answer like "clean out the pantry" (admittedly, a pretty weird answer). At other times, I may want to take a nap, go for a jog, visit a bookshop, or just sit and relax.

As creative beings—and we all are—we need periods in which to live spontaneously without commitments or distractions. By creating space to live in the moment, we strengthen the connection to our inner wisdom and give ourselves a much-needed rest from the routine of day-to-day living. If the daily routine is getting the better of you, it may be time for you to play.

Task 1: Play dates

Get your diary and schedule a play date with yourself—now! Go on! Make time in your life for a spontaneous pamper break. Take an afternoon off from appointments and, if you have kids, book them in with their grandparents or another trusted babysitter for a sleepover and free yourself from obligations.

During your play time, check in with your wise self and ask, "What do I really want to do right now?" However goofy the response is, just do it and have fun doing it.

Task 2: Having fun

One night I was in the car with my son and an ABBA song came on the radio that reminded me of when I was young. On a whim, I grabbed my son by the arm and we pretended to be in the band while driving home. My son was on guitar and back-up vocals and I was the lead singer. This behavior is very unlike me as I can be quite serious most of the time. Singing to my heart's content with my son reminded me how important it is to be silly and act like a child when we live in a busy adult world. So pretend you are the lead singer of your favorite band and sing as loudly as you can!

I always know when fun is missing from my daily diet when the very mention of the word "fun," annoys me. Doing something out of the ordinary can be a great way to add some fun to your life.

On the spirit of child's play, here are some tips to help your inner little one come out to play. Pick one action and do it each week. You may be pleasantly surprised at how much joy this gives you.

- Buy yourself a giant pad of paper (or butcher paper) and some crayons and schedule in your diary a time to draw, scribble, or use your fingers to smudge colors together.
- Invite friends over for a meal and forget the silverware. Have your guests eat with their hands (serve spaghetti to make it really fun).
- Buy several tins of Play-Doh® and keep them in your office. Create a new Play-Doh® monster each week and sit it on your desk.
- Spend an hour in the forest or at the beach, and notice the color of the trees or ocean and shells you see that make for forest and ocean jewels.
- Close the curtains, put on your favorite music, and dance in your living room.
- Get dirty. Go out and weed in the garden, plant a tree, or simply dig holes for fun!
- Spend time on a swing at your local park after work and eat an ice cream.
- Buy a Hula-Hoop and see if you can still swing your hips.
- Get a semi-permanent tattoo.
- Paint your partner's toenails bright pink.
- Have a serious conversation with your pet.
- Visit a toy shop and buy a coloring-in book. Take it to work with you and spend fifteen minutes each day coloring it in.
- Grab your or your neighbor's kids and take them to the local fair. While you're there, get your faces painted.

- Grab a watermelon and have a competition to see who can spit the seeds the farthest distance.
- Raid your children's dress-up box and play with them. Seeing the world through children's eyes is truly magical and inspiring.

For some of you, engaging in any of the above activities list will be daunting and you may feel silly or uncomfortable. But don't skip this part. Make your own list (after all, play for you is different to play for the next person). The rewards of choosing this action will deliver untold magic to you.

Task 3: Sitting still

Because we live in a fast-paced society and we are often "stuck" in our headspace, being hurried and disconnected, and feeling overwhelmed by a huge to-do list, you need a way to help you connect with the energy in your body beyond meditation and yoga.

Your task is to sit quietly, even if it's just for five minutes a day. Eventually you will feel the vibration of your own body just by sitting still. You'll start to notice that you actually have a vibrational frequency around your body.

If you sit in that space, you can make a decision to strengthen that energy field around you. You will also come to recognize, when you first start practicing this, that most likely you feel incredibly constricted; you might pulsate in a very constricted way as opposed to being fluid and free flowing.

You can also take it a step further. If energy is louder than words—and I believe that it is—it therefore follows that energy is also more powerful than words. If you really want to get a message across, get in touch with what your energy is saying and projecting as opposed to the words that are coming out of your mouth, because they can be poles apart. If that's the case, you won't get the results that you want.

The best way to check in on what your energy is doing is asking yourself, "What am I feeling? How do I feel in my body today?" Be aware of what feelings, emotions, and belief systems are affecting your energy supply. If you want to know what your energy is doing in the world, look at people's responses to you. Look at how people behave toward you. Look at what life is delivering to you. Then you'll recognize what you're creating or not creating.

Your affirmation for kidding around

"Play time boosts my ability to enjoy my life!"

Your daily must-do

The process of change is made more powerful and meaningful when we commit to raising our level of positivity each day. And as you know, we can easily kick-start this process by starting our day with the negative "mind chatter" dump.

Your review

1. What were my personal highlights during this energetic phase?
2. What challenges did I face and how did I handle them?
3. What exciting new insights did I discover about myself?

4. What was my greatest achievement in this phase?
5. What is my commitment for the next phase?

Remember

By the end of this book, you will discover what inspires you and who you want to be—and then you'll achieve it.

Your checklist

A. Complete Task 1: Play dates.
B. Complete Task 2: Having fun.
C. Complete Task 3: Sitting still.
D. Write out affirmation and verbalize daily.
E. Daily must-do: "mind chatter" dump.
F. Complete review.

THOUGHTS

It's important to spend time with a piece of paper and a pen and ask yourself: What do I think? What do I believe in? What are my thoughts and opinions around relationships, money, career, life in general? What do I value in my life? What are the qualities that I want to look for here?

There is power and truth in knowing what you think. Don't be afraid of sitting down and spending time getting to know your deep inner thoughts, because those deep inner thoughts and your belief systems are designing and creating your life as you know it now.

Your life is where it is right now because of the thoughts and the beliefs that you've held about yourself. There is no other reason, no other excuse. No one else has designed your life except you. You are one hundred percent responsible for the state of your life and it's because of the thoughts that you hold about yourself. Your beliefs and your values—your thoughts about what your life should be—are crucial in determining how your life will change and if, in fact, it will change. For example, if you believe you want to have a certain type of job, a job that brings you a lot of money but also takes up most of your time, and your values—such as wanting to spend more time with your family—are at odds with this belief, it will be impossible for you to achieve any kind of change, let alone the change you want. In this chapter we will look closely at what you believe and what you value, and whether they are compatible.

When I was quite young, I remember Mom suddenly not being at home anymore to look after my brother and me after school. It hit me with a feeling of just being left; there was definitely, from my point of view, a sense of abandonment. The person that I loved most in life was no longer there to talk to about my day as soon as I came home. Instead, Mom was at work, with quite long hours, and my brother and I were looked after by a lovely neighbor whose wonderful, nurturing care was just what I needed at the time.

I'd watch Mom work really hard at her job, then come home and look after a husband and two kids, cook, clean, and keep our home in immaculate order. I don't really recall my father helping out around the house, and some of this I can perhaps write off to generational norms of the time, but I just think that I saw Mom being superwoman. Witnessing my mother work so hard created beliefs in my mind that I wanted a greater sense of freedom, choice, and balance when I had a family and a career. I didn't want the fatigue and resentment. I knew that my parents' marriage was unhappy and there were times when she really threw herself into her career as a means of escaping dealing with some of those issues. Basically, my beliefs were that men didn't help out around the house; it was down to women to do all the housework and child-rearing and be available to work outside the home as well, and be great at all of it!

I really struggled with these beliefs for a long time, to the point of physical collapse; I questioned my values and expectations about roles that I had absorbed from my childhood, examples that had been set by my parents. I found myself in conflict between what I wanted from life (more balance and more time with my child) versus the lifestyles that my parents had shown me (hard work to the point of exhaustion, perfection with no room for failure, and imbalance in the domestic roles). Who was I to question my parents? What did I know?

The tension within myself was high. Ideally, I wanted a satisfying career that would allow me to be truly present in my son's life—be around for his reading classes, help out at the school lunch box duty, pick him up from school every day. And, of course, I longed for a caring and supportive partner, someone who would actually share the cooking and cleaning and washing with me, not just assume that these domestic chores were somehow my sole responsibility as a woman.

I suffered through years of stress over what I was taught versus what I sought. Ultimately, I resolved it by following my heart and realizing that for me, being a hands-on mom was so important that building a satisfying career that allowed me to be available to my son would provide the balance between work and home that I had always craved.

Beliefs

Whenever I want to find a solution to a problem, I usually get the best result when I step away from the problem. I then take some time to consider what I was actually thinking about the problem, what I believed about the problem, and whether or not my values line up with my beliefs about the issue at hand. The more time I used to spend worrying about a certain event, the chances were good that my thoughts would match my outcome in a negative manner. It was only when I created space to review my thoughts that I could see where the real challenge was needed.

Let me give you a real life example. Just before I went through my own coaching, I was working in a corporate job for a multinational company. I was earning great money and achieved career successes, yet I was bored. Part of me was also starting to think I was unworthy of the job and completely ungrateful. I had a job that people would kill for and here I was just going through the motions because it was unfulfilling. This feeling of not really being where I wanted to be career-wise was one of the leading reasons that I sought out coaching. I knew I wanted to do something else, but I wasn't sure how to get there and I was worried about changing to a job that might not offer the financial security that I wanted, the hours that I wanted (by this stage, I was a new mom), and be in the city that I wanted to be in. I was really starting to spiral into a negative thought pattern about changing jobs.

During the coaching process, not only did I realize that I needed to stop thinking that I was virtually unemployable but I needed to give myself the grace to create some space in my mindset to realign my thoughts about who I was, what I was capable of achieving, and where I wanted to go professionally. I spent almost a year with my life coach figuring out who I was and what I wanted to become, and by the time I had been through my own coaching I knew that this was what I wanted to do full-time.

I had applied some time and space around my thinking, and I found a path forward that would offer me a career and a lifestyle that would make me very happy indeed.

If you really want transformation in your life, you must change how you live and how you think. To do that, you need to know what it is you're actually thinking in the first place and what it is that you believe about yourself.

Overcoming limiting beliefs

There are ways and methods that can be used to overcome any limiting beliefs you have and change the way you look at your negative beliefs in a more positive and productive way, forever.

There are also some important distinctions to be made about how we change our beliefs or limiting decisions. Your beliefs have been created by what you have absorbed over the years from a parent, the education system, the government, friends, family, society, and so on. Some of these beliefs are driven by unconscious fears that you may not even be aware of.

If you are unhappy with a part of your life, this is when belief-changing is key. For most of us, we are caught up in the day-to-day pace of life and we believe that things just happen to us, rather than spending time breaking down this notion and looking at it from the wider perspective of how we are contributing to, or creating, what is happening to us. The idea that we are contributing to, or creating, our realities can be viewed both positively and negatively. Clearly, we want to remedy the negative thinking and bring it all around to a much more positive perspective.

One of the key areas that I had to focus on when I was doing this exercise (and even today I still refer back to it, when I'm not feeling in tip-top form) was my belief around not being good enough. I won't lie—there are days when this negative thought does enter my head, but I'm old enough and wise enough to know that I have the tools to break this belief down. I go through my five dimensions to find out where this thought is sitting, and I start working through any roadblocks that I might be experiencing.

The first thing I usually turn to is the physical. How do I feel? Is this just a matter of going for a long walk on the beach to change up my energy and get moving? How's my diet? Have I been eating foods that don't agree with me? Then I turn to other areas. Have I fallen out of alignment with my dimension of spirituality? Have I been meditating and praying enough lately? You get the point. I just go through the list and see where the alignment is a bit off and I start doing the things that I know work for me. Some days are easier to get it all together than others, but I do get it together and I am always grateful that I do, because getting that alignment just right makes all the difference.

In transforming a negative core belief, it is necessary to first look at the particular belief, its origins, and what sort of force it has in your whole life. Listed below are some common negative thoughts that people have on a daily basis. Yours might be different, yet no less limiting.

Some common negative thoughts

- I am not good enough
- I am unlovable
- I am controlling
- I am needy
- I don't deserve much
- I am too much
- I am stupid
- I am fat

- I am a loser
- My body is frail
- Relationships are difficult
- I need a good education to get a good job
- Money doesn't grow on trees
- Men are useless around the house
- I don't have enough time
- Young people are bad drivers
- I deserve to be alone
- I don't deserve to be happy.

As you become more aware of your negative thought patterns and your reactions and responses, understand that you can choose to change them. This new awareness also gives you insights into areas of your life in which these beliefs and patterns have been keeping you hostage. By acknowledging the areas in which you are holding negative beliefs and then shedding an understanding light on them, you are making the decision to create change and take action. Try to face this awareness with compassion and kindness. It's not the end of the world—it's only the beginning, as you realize the limiting beliefs that no longer serve you.

Task 1: Finding the truth

The objective of this easy-to-follow exercise is to help replace negative and limiting thoughts and beliefs about yourself with positive and empowering ones. If you have any area in your life in which the same type of problem repeats time and again (as most of us do), this is a good indication that you're harboring some negative core beliefs in that area.

Doing this once a week, you will examine these areas and begin the process of eliminating the erroneous core beliefs that have been creating the problems.

Give yourself ten minutes to complete this exercise.

1. Study the list below and check the items that correspond to areas in your life which are frequently problematic:

    - Career
    - Family relationships
    - Committed relationships
    - Feelings of inferiority
    - Indecisiveness
    - Fear
    - Physical health
    - Personal security
    - Business
    - Monetary supply
    - Friendships
    - Work relationships
    - Feelings of superiority
    - Lack of direction or focus
    - Unhappiness/depression
    - Physical image
    - Living environment
    - Community/government.

2. Now make sure you are sitting comfortably. Close your eyes and contemplate the area or areas you have indicated. Ask your inner wisdom to shine its brilliant white light of truth throughout your consciousness. Visualize this

white light shining into every nook and cranny of your consciousness. See it light up all the dark pockets. Let this light shine upon every core belief.

3. Go deeply inside your heart and ask for any message to come forward. Ask your heart to present anything that you should deal with. Ask yourself: "Do I have any self-limiting beliefs? What are my actual beliefs and what might simply be assumptions?"

4. When you are ready, open your eyes again and grab a pen and paper and note down any ideas that have come up during your reflection process.

5. Say and write these new beliefs twenty times a day to start reprogramming a new way of thinking and being. These will become your true beliefs; they are what you think. I recommend you read them daily and remind yourself when you're driving, washing up, and so on of what you now hold to be true for you.

It may help you to place Post-It® notes around the house, write in your diary, make a note in your phone—anywhere that will help you to remember the new state you want to experience. If you write down your positive comments, quotes, and affirmations and put them around the house where you can see them, you will start to see positive changes.

Your affirmation for changing core beliefs

"I am open to a new, positive way of thinking, and new opportunities are unfolding in my life right now."

Your daily must-do

By now, I'm sure that you've found your groove with the "mind chatter" dump and you might even be enjoying the change that it's brought to your life. I'm hoping that you've found this to be an enriching exercise and not a chore, that it has helped to bring you clarity and freedom of thought and allowed you to reach higher levels of positivity as you continue the practice.

Your review

1. What were my personal highlights during this intellectual phase?
2. What challenges did I face and how did I handle them?
3. What exciting new insights did I discover about myself?
4. What was my greatest achievement in this phase?
5. What is my commitment for the next phase?

Remember

By the end of this book, you will discover what inspires you and who you want to be—and then you'll achieve it.

Your checklist

A. Complete Task 1: Finding the truth.
B. Write out affirmation and verbalize daily.
C. Daily must-do: "mind chatter" dump.
D. Complete review.

CHECKING IN

Before you move on, now is a good opportunity to revisit some of the tasks and tools that I recommend you use constantly. These tools will help you check in with where you're at and whether you're ready to move on.

Roadblock exercise

As you work through this book, you will keep confronting roadblocks. This is a normal part of the process. The following exercise will help you move through those roadblocks—you don't want to move around them because then they'll still be there! There is a way to move through any roadblock.

Write down the answers to the following questions, either in this book or in your journal.

Outcomes

What are the outcomes I am seeking in life?

1. _____

2. _____

3. _____

What am I stating I want in my life that I never seem to create?

    1. _____

    2. _____

    3. _____

Is this clear and am I clear about how it looks and feels?

_____

Actions

What are the actions I am taking toward this?

    1. _____

    2. _____

    3. _____

Do I act in alignment with my outcome?

_____

What action am I taking right now that is not in alignment with my outcome?

    1. _____

    2. _____

    3. _____

Thoughts

- What am I thinking about myself, my actions and the outcome?
- My thoughts create my reality so are they in alignment with my actions and my outcome?
- What words am I speaking?
- Do they match my actions and outcome?
- If not, what changes can I make which will support my outcome and goals?
- What three things can I start to do differently today toward my outcomes?
- What three things can I think differently toward my outcomes?
- What words can I speak that will contribute to me creating my outcomes?

The Manifestation Tool

Let's refresh the Manifestation Tool. It contains your steps for change.

My purpose + thoughts + vision + my words + feelings + actions + gratitude = goal.

It may be helpful for you to do the Manifestation Tool exercise again, as this tool is critical for the creation of the life you will love. Ideally, you will have this tool constantly in mind as you work through each chapter, but just in case you need a refresher, go back to page 167.

As a tip, I generally make use of the Manifestation Tool when I'm redefining my goals, or I feel a little like I'm off track with some of things I'm needing in life. It's a great reminder to just set things right and clear my thoughts.

Affirmations

It's also a good time to review the affirmations you have been working with. In addition to the affirmation given in each chapter, you should be working with general affirmations for your life, as we covered in the Affirmations chapter.

Are these affirmations still appropriate? Do you need to adjust them to reflect the changes you have already gone through? Refer back to this chapter as needed.

Visualizations

Visualizations are fun. They create excitement and put energy into creating the new changes you desire and you can practice visualizations as often as you like. Here's a visualization technique that I like to use.

The movie of your life

Imagine you're sitting in your favorite cinema, all cozy in a comfortable seat. You're looking at your life playing out on the big screen. That's right: watch yourself act out all the new changes you want to have happen in your life. It may be a new job, new partner, wealth, health … Whatever it is you want in your life, I invite you to imagine what this looks like and put it on the big screen.

What does this look like? What clothes are you wearing? What is the location? What are you saying? Do you have a smile on your face? Get up close and personal with this blockbuster movie of you. Look at the big screen and actually see yourself living the change, knowing that you are the writer of this movie's script and you can change the scenes as you go along.

This is a fun exercise to do each day. Try doing it when you're in the shower or lying in bed—the best time to do it is before you start your day. Putting energy into this exercise helps to anchor your thoughts to the new you. If you can't see the details, you need to do some further work to help you be crystal clear on what this new change looks like. It may be that you're not ready to watch this movie, but don't worry—you will be.

Guided visualizations

There are so many different visualizations you can do. My favorite is the movie, but there are many fantastic offerings on YouTube, or podcasts that offer guided visualizations that you can listen to when you are resting and have some quiet time for yourself. (Please don't do these visualizations while driving the car!) For those who want to listen to a guided visualization, there are some steps to follow:

1. Clear your mind. Most of us have so many thoughts going on in our heads that it's impossible to focus intently. To succeed in anything new, you need to be able to focus your mind. Without focus, you can't perform at your best or properly get the benefits and value from creative visualizations. So then, surrender all other thoughts and concerns. Nothing else exists during your visualization but you and the voice on the guided visualization.

2. Establish the vision, or your movie! To get what you want, you need to know what it is, so before you press "play", write down all the things you think you want. Don't edit yourself; just get it all down on paper. Keep writing. After a few minutes, you will have a complete list. Now choose one item from that list that's most important right now. You can go for the others later.

3. Record the details. Once you have your item from the list, define it in detail. Become clear about what you want. If it's a new car, state the brand, the color, the model year and the major upgrades it has, such as its leather interior. Specifics are very important. You want it to feel so real—as though it's already in your possession.

4. Rewrite and refine. Once you've got it down, it's time to shape your description into something closer to exactly what it is you want. This creative visualization technique is like taking a rough idea of what you want to say in a letter-to-the-editor and then converting it into a polished piece that's ready to mail. Refine your goal into a powerful paragraph that describes exactly what it is you want.

FEELINGS

In this chapter, we take a look at the personal and intimate experiences that have more than likely left an emotional mark on your heart. You will explore your emotional difficulties and undertake to heal the shame of past failures. You will gain compassion for yourself as you learn from your wounds and dismantle the emotional blocks from the past, creating a renewed sense of learning and growth.

We all have a story, a script that we've written about who and what we are, and we all tend to stick to it—no matter what. Most of us tend to have a narrative that is founded on fear and trauma because, let's face it, who hasn't struggled with fear, trauma, and self-esteem issues?

However, when we spend some time with ourselves uncovering who we are and what is important to us, and are operating from a place of compassion, forgiveness, honesty, and vulnerability, we are able to see our story for what it is, just a story, one that we have control over and can rewrite, reframe, and move forward with at any time. We come to understand that we are not small in the story of our life; we are actually the hero and we have the freedom, choice, and power over how our story is propelled forward. You can be a victim to your story or you can become victorious. The way you become victorious through your story is by understanding it, practicing forgiveness where that needs to happen, letting the unimportant go, and then making decisions and having actions that back up what you want your new story to look like.

As the writer of your story, it's entirely up to you how many backpacks full of burden you wish to carry around with you for the rest of your life. Experience tells me that as the years progress, those backpacks just get filled with more and more negativity, emotional clutter, and mental anguish that make it impossible to keep moving forward if you don't stop and make a full assessment of what is really going on. You need to take control of your story and ask yourself what you need to let go of, what you need to accept, what you need to find forgiveness for, and where you haven't been loving enough of yourself as a result of your story. I also believe that you've had the story you've had for a reason, and you can learn from it. There's a reason why you've chosen to journey down the path that you have.

There have been times in my life when I've had to revisit my story and do a full analysis to break it down to see where I've been holding on to negativity that isn't serving me. Twenty years ago, I was a great big victim in my own story! True. I had the most elaborate and justifiable limiting mindsets that you could dream up and I was constantly wondering why I wasn't getting ahead. I would tell myself I wasn't good enough, I wasn't lovable, I didn't deserve love. There were a lot of limiting beliefs, but I took a deep breath and really looked at who I was and what I was telling myself. The point here is that your story will be confronting, but don't stop. On the other side awaits a life you'll love and it's absolutely worth the journey. When you spend time doing your story in this chapter, you will find it incredibly disconcerting because you'll see a part of you that you've been unwilling to see. But a story is just a story. And the story will only have an impact on your life if you let it.

The importance of your life story

Several years ago, before I had the advantage of training as a coach and applying the skills to my own life, I struggled with the concept of realizing that what was missing from my life was, in fact, myself. I tried to change on the outside in an effort to convince myself that my life was different—that I was different. But it only ended up in further despair and depression. When I finally had enough of playing out the same movie over and over, I was ready to roll up my sleeves and get serious about changing the path my life was on. One of the things that helped me was to completely stop and re-evaluate how I was living my life and how I spent my time with myself and others. I took a deep breath, pressed pause on my life, and proceeded to dismantle the negative script with kindness about who I was and where I was at.

If you feel there are aspects of your life where you are not being completely truthful with yourself, now's the time to be gentle and honest as you make your way through your re-evaluation. Sometimes it can be very painful to dispel the myths surrounding who you are and how upholding these illusions have impacted your life. However, you are now firmly planted in the realm of choice—you can choose from this moment forward to do things differently or not, but you can no longer avoid the fact that you have reached an apex of change.

Changing your story

Most of us are completely unaware that we live the same story day after day. We are so caught up in our story that we are blissfully ignorant to the hand we had in creating it. Are you aware that you create the same patterns and situations in your life—your "stories"—but that they are often masked by different characters or actors?

You may change jobs only to find that you work for the same type of boss who annoys you and makes you feel useless. You may change boyfriends and realize after a short while that you are in bed with the same man—only this one has brown hair. You may move to a different city only to find that you attract the same types of friends who want rescuing. Have you noticed how many of us change jobs, relationships, where we live, our hair color, and think that it will fill that internal void? Yet we continue to be challenged by the same old story again, and again, and again.

For some people, change is addictive: they do lots of it because it makes them feel like they're moving ahead in life. Other people believe that changes on the outside will instantaneously change them on the inside. In both cases, these are cosmetic or superficial changes. The same story or pattern is continuing, and the real, structural, foundational change that needs to occur on the inside has been overlooked and ignored. Understandably, deep investigation of oneself is challenging and people generally avoid doing it out of fear that they might have to look at things they really don't like. However, as you take stock of yourself and uncover some things that are disagreeable, you're equally as likely to see some lovely things that have been taken for granted for far too long. Take heart and forge ahead with bravery and kindness because it's not all hard work, and greatness awaits you.

At this point, you have a choice: you can either start to see the power of your story or pretend it is not a problem for you and continue to create the same old patterns and scenarios. Maybe you want to step back and look at your life from a symbolic perspective: you will realize that you are the main character in a fabulous drama that would make a wonderful movie.

Change is usually difficult, and most of us resist it. Instead of inviting change into their lives, most people would rather ignore the physical signs of unhappiness like feeling tired all the time, bad digestion, and a sore back, and the non-physical signs like a poor relationship history, believing that everything is someone else's fault, "accidents just happen," feeling disconnected from the world and having constant money worries. For many people, that is just life and they feel powerless to change. Moreover, they don't know if they really want to change it, because at a certain point, even though life is difficult and disappointing, the difficulty and disappointment is a known quantity and therefore more easily acceptable.

What usually makes people want to change their story and to change the patterns of their lives is that they reach a critical point where they can no longer cope with any more pain. Until they reach this point, they will continue to run the same old movie, just swapping the main characters every so often. But pain is an amazing change agent. It can help you start to identify your role in your life and what you continue to create in your life, so you can then start looking deep within and activating change on the inside of you.

Once you actively choose to look at your patterns of behavior and at the stories that keep you stuck, only then will you create an external environment that mirrors the internal world within you.

Task 1: Working through the years

Using the structure given below, write down the story of your life, highlighting all the poignant moments, pivotal experiences, tragedy, and trauma. This is clearly quite a big task, and one that you should spend some time on. It's asking a lot from you on so many levels. I've taken some time to reveal my own personal insights that I recall from these stages in my life, and I offer them to you as an example.

0–5 years of age

- What experiences can I recall at this age?

   There's not a lot that I remember from being this young, but the things that do spring to mind are a feeling of anxiety and aloneness, a real sense of being left alone by myself, and helplessness. I was a very young child and had no idea of how to fend for myself, take care of myself, and this all made me feel decidedly on edge, all the time.

   Arguments. I remember arguments and angry words between my parents. Not what they said, but that feeling of tension in the air and there being no safe place when everyone was upset.

- How did I feel?

   The tension within the household made me feel anxious most of the time, just this overall sense of things not being well, or right, or settled. It was like all the oxygen had escaped the house when I was at home. I didn't feel safe or comfortable, yet I knew nothing else so I began to absorb these feelings as normal. The sense of abandonment was strong and really contributed to my general unease at home. I felt like I was so small that I was virtually invisible.

- What beliefs did I take on?

  These early childhood experiences and feelings told me that I wasn't important; that I didn't count in the world and my voice could not, and more importantly would not, be recognized or heard.

- In what ways did my experiences impact me later in life, both positive and negative?

  As I worked my way through my teens and into early adulthood, I sought validation in the outside world in my career, my relationships, anything that I believed would bring me recognition and therefore make me feel important and worthwhile. The downside to this kind of behavior is that, once the external source of validation is removed, your self-esteem evaporates. The only real validation that is beneficial is internal: discovering and nurturing what you love about yourself and disregarding belief systems that hold you hostage to a life you don't want.

5–10 years of age

- What experiences can I recall at this age?

  I remember abuse, betrayal, and lies, all huge things for a young child to operate under the weight of and not have the words or ability to make sense of. My world was entirely based on destabilization.

- How did I feel?

    My world at this stage was completely internal and frenetic. I had no understanding of the dysfunctionality of the duality that I was living with, the vast gap between what I was seeing and what I was feeling with zero resolution in sight. I was isolated, filled with sadness, and suffering excruciating emotional pain and turmoil. I was struggling to make sense of the experiences occurring with my father and learning to engage in a life of secrecy.

- What beliefs did I take on?

    I lived with the beliefs that I was of little importance in the world, that my pain was unseen, my feelings utterly redundant, and that I could trust no one. My main objective was survival, and it was all instinct because I lacked the very skills I needed to be able to protect myself.

- In what ways did my experiences impact me later in life, both positive and negative?

    In later life, I developed an uncanny ability to attract destructive relationships that mirrored my inner turmoil. Even when I did meet someone who was kind and loving, I was so injured by my experiences that I was unable to recognize what healthy and loving actually looked like. My heart had been so wounded that it shut down completely with an iron lock that I would not allow any access to.

10–15 years of age

- What experiences can I recall at this age?

  I spent my early teenage years perpetrating the typical acts of rebellion and avoiding being at home. I stayed out late with my friends, I flirted with drinking and boys, and I most definitely refused to listen to any adults in my life. It was self-sabotaging behavior coming from a place of enormous pain and discomfort.

- How did I feel?

  Not only did I feel out of control, I was out of control. I had no sense of equanimity or boundaries and I literally felt rudderless. I was a perpetual ball of frustration, angst, pain, and urgency.

- What beliefs did I take on?

  I began to believe that I was destined for a life of struggle and pressure from which I could not escape. I believed that no one could see me and that therefore I would remain misunderstood for the rest of my life, that I was the only person that could protect my feelings and reliance on others was a complete waste of time. My unsettled internal feelings played out in the belief that it was impossible to get away from my family.

- In what ways did my experiences impact me later in life, both positive and negative?

  When I sought out relationships later on, I did so with an underlying need to feel safe. I looked for a partner who would provide me the familial stability that I had not had as a child. I was looking for that person to give me everything that I had missed out on, and that was a truly flawed foundation for any relationship.

At this point in my life, I had come up with a plan to leave home as soon as I possibly could. I needed to flee from the pain. I was both terrified and angry, but I was also hopeful that something better lay ahead. Planning my escape gave me a sense of independence and strength. And I can see now that my experiences forged my resiliency and ability to be self-reliant.

15–20 years of age

- What experiences can I recall at this age?

    Like a lot of kids this age, I struggled with friendships, with school itself, and my sense of belonging. I felt outside of, and estranged from, those around me and I was entirely focused on leaving home as soon as school was finished.

- How did I feel?

    I was filled with the anticipation of my soon-to-be-lived freedom. I was both scared and excited in equal measure, and antsy to be out on my own and living life by my own rules.

- What beliefs did I take on?

    I was still very much operating in survival mode, believing that I could only rely on myself and that trusting anyone on any deep level was simply not an option. Help from others was not going to be forthcoming, and who was I to even believe that I deserved it?

- In what ways did my experiences impact me later in life, both positive and negative?

  Positively, my childhood experiences and beliefs showed me that I could dig deep within myself to find solutions and build an independent life away from my unhappy home, that I had the power within.

  Negatively, I was unable to trust anyone or let people help me. I kept the world at arm's length and presented a superficially happy and successful facade. Keeping people distanced made me feel safe, yet I was deeply alone, felt invisible, and ultimately unlovable.

20–30 years of age

- What experiences can I recall at this age?

  During my twenties, I spent a number of years navigating relationships that mirrored my lack of self-worth and self-esteem. I attracted men who didn't treat me with love or respect, who lied to me, cheated on me, and were bullies.

  In my career, I was striving to prove myself to myself. I worked hard and had incredible opportunities that allowed me to grow, travel the world, excel, and make a difference in the lives of others.

  I was also embarking on my own journey of self-discovery through coaching that would see me begin to tackle my own mess and then start my new career in coaching.

  At twenty-eight, I suffered a bout of meningitis that I thought had been caused by overwork, stress, and a simple lack of adequately taking care of myself. In hindsight, I now see that my body was telling me that I was living too much in my own head, and was completely disconnected from my heart and soul, and utterly out of balance in all respects of life.

- How did I feel?

I swung wildly between feeling confident and empowered to feeling bereft and isolated. Unable to find a relationship that would offer me the security and stability I yearned for, I sank further into unhappiness and feelings of aloneness. Upon reflection, I can now clearly see that I was unconsciously looking for an appropriate father figure in my life. I was trying to find a lover who would provide to me feelings of appropriate care, love, and emotional nourishment.

- What beliefs did I take on?

I believed that I was stuck in a life of unhappiness, that I was alone, and that no one could love me, let alone understand me. I truly believed that the feelings I had at that point in my life would never leave me and that this was all I was capable of in terms of my emotions.

- In what ways did my experiences impact me later in life, both positive and negative?

I actively avoided emotional intimacy during this time, keeping all my relationships superficial and shallow, thus not allowing anyone to wound me. I also held the expectation that anyone in my immediate circle should be able to know what I was thinking and feeling, that I didn't need to tell them. They were adults and they should know. I believed that I should be rescued, that I could be rescued and saved by other people.

What I ultimately came to learn is that I had the power to rescue myself from my unhappiness, that the key to my life is actually self-love, and from there abundance in all its forms flows.

Throughout my thirties and forties, I worked hard on myself, breaking down bad habits and understanding how my life works at its best, to achieve transformation, balance and happiness. I have learned that it really doesn't matter how old you are, but rather what you think and believe about yourself that is important. Your opinion is the only opinion that really matters; after all, you are the one that has to sleep with your own conscience. It takes courage to look at yourself with clear eyes, at your belief systems, and your life experiences, and turn them into pillars that will support you to build a life you love.

As I approach midlife in my fifties, I have realized that it's taken the best part of a couple of decades to finally integrate all the varied parts of my life's journey and feel whole. Not everyone will have experienced the extremes of my story; however, the purpose of this book, and my life's work, is for you to understand that regardless of your history, experiences, and beliefs, you are able to redefine and rechart your course. It most definitely takes a healthy dose of bravery to confront and hold yourself accountable for the past, the present, and the future, but a life based on self-love and self-validation awaits you when you do.

Task 2: Patterns

Now that you have written down what has happened in the past, you will be able to identify any patterns such as abandonment, rejection, avoidance, addictive behavior, sadness, and depression. Write down the answers to the following questions and be brutally honest with yourself. No one else needs to know what you've written, so you don't have to hide anything.

What belief systems am I still playing out in my life?

1. _____

2. _____

3. _____

4. _____

5. _____

How are they impacting my life currently?

1. _____

2. _____

3. _____

4. _____

5. _____

Hello Coach!

What do I need to let go of in my life that is holding me back from success?

1. _____
2. _____
3. _____
4. _____
5. _____

What awareness did I learn that would help me move forward and make different choices?

1. _____
2. _____
3. _____
4. _____
5. _____

Do I need extra support (for example, therapy, body work, kinesiology) to shift childhood beliefs that I feel may be preventing me from creating success in my life? If so, they are:

1. _____
2. _____
3. _____

4. _____

5. _____

Your affirmation for your life story

"I consciously release the past and live only in the present. That way, I get to enjoy and experience life to the full."

Your daily must-do

Just a gentle reminder that doing your daily negative "mind chatter" dump is increasing your capacity to letting positive thoughts flow into you.

Fear

Let's take a look at fears and what they can be, as there are many ways to view how a fear can affect your life.

Fear can lead us to making the right choices, but it is the debilitating effects of unjustified or irrational fear that we want to bring to light. How can we eliminate the fear that prevents us from reaching our potential? It starts with awareness. Although we may have no control over the events or circumstances that we fear, our anxiety does not need to be part of those events. Our fear is merely a reflection of how we interpret those events.

Like most people, I have fears—fears surrounding my friends and loved ones, fears around my health. But what keeps me in check is my reliance on the tools that I use—the five dimensions to realign my thinking. When I am anxious about the results of a medical check-up, I think about what else is going on in my life that might be manifesting itself as a fear of the check-up. Perhaps I'm fearing the results because I haven't been as physically active as I know I should be. Perhaps I've been working too many late nights in a row and not sleeping well and am feeling particularly fatigued because I've set myself an arbitrary work deadline. None of these things necessarily mean that I'll be having a health crisis, but they can be a trigger for getting my mind racing and thinking that the worst is about to happen.

Once I slow myself down and look at all the surrounding elements in my life that are causing me to feel fearful, I'm able to disassemble them and make a plan for finding some more balance and getting out of that negative thought pattern.

Your fear is composed of your thoughts

When we accept and take responsibility for that fact that fear is only a manifestation of our own thoughts, we can begin to unravel those fears and make steps toward positive progress.

Sometimes we cleverly hide our fears by disguising them. If we want to root them out, we need to be mindful of our thoughts and carefully analyze them. For example, when I say that I would prefer to remain in my present job because I am a cautious person, it may really mean that I am afraid to change jobs. Similarly, when I say that I'm not interested in computers, I may really be saying that I'm afraid of computers because I don't understand how to use them. These are examples of fears masquerading themselves as limiting beliefs that we are allowing to rule our lives. By acknowledging that they are dressed up fears that can be remedied by making a concentrated effort to step away from those fears and limitations, we consciously and systematically make forward movement toward our goal. And not only that, the pure relief of having shed that baggage empowers us toward embracing joy and living confidently in the life that we love.

Moving out of fear

The good news around fear is that there is a cure! And that cure is action. You don't need to be overwhelmed by fear, and you don't necessarily need to take action on a grand scale. Indeed, by taking on too much too soon and taking giant steps away from your fears, you may inadvertently fail to overcome what scares you, and this could see you backsliding and growing less confident in your abilities. My recommendation is that you need to take small, manageable, baby steps, and that's just what we'll do with the exercises in this chapter.

As you take these small steps, each success will encourage and motivate you to continue. The rewards are well worth it. If you are wondering where to start, it's simple: get involved with life. Learn as much as you can. Develop curiosity. Men and women have risked their lives boarding rockets and space shuttles not because they are reckless or fearless, but because they are curious. They are explorers yearning to go where few have ever been. You, too, can become an explorer. You can explore your vast universe of inner space. You can plunge into the depths of your being and discover the courage to chart a new life, a new beginning. Resolve to live the life of your dreams right now. Kick down the barriers of fear and venture into the unknown.

Dare to discover your hidden powers. Your imagination is like a powerful magnet that draws to it whatever you are anticipating.

If you are expecting a bright and sunny life, lo and behold, that's exactly what you get. But if all you expect from life are dark clouds and gloom, prepare for storms for they will surely come. When you use your imagination to focus on the positive, it's an empowering and liberating experience. When you use it to focus on the negative, it's a paralyzing and crippling experience. And anticipation of fear can lead to explosive tension.

Become sensitive to your feelings. When you are aware of them, you can control them rather than have them control you. When you feel afraid of doing something you should be doing, stare fear in the face. Say, "I am not afraid of you. I welcome and embrace you. But it is I, not you, who will decide what I am afraid of. I welcome fear. I welcome you, fear, as a friend, for you always point the way I can experience more growth."

From now on, whenever you feel fear, pause to discover the lesson it's bringing you: is it to avoid danger or to accept a new challenge?

I do want to make a disclaimer here about fear of real danger. When I talk about fear, I'm talking about limiting self-beliefs that stop us from growing. I am not referring to real, threatening danger from someone or something that could genuinely hurt you. In those instances, you should seek legitimate help from people such as the police or medical experts. If you are in any sort of jeopardy that will cause you harm that could result in tragic circumstances, please remedy it appropriately.

Task 3: Overcoming fear

The objective of this exercise is to teach you to overcome fear.

1. In your journal, list the fears you believe are active in your life.

    - Once you've listed the fears, rank them in order of greatest intensity, with number one being the worst fear. If you're having difficulty with this exercise—it's genuinely confronting—try moving into it by referring to these areas of your life—physical, emotional, spiritual, financial, career, friends, and family.
    - Rank your fears in these categories on a scale of one to ten; one being the scariest, ten being the least scary. There's no need to reach ten, just what you feel is an active and current fear in your own life right now.

2. Once you have ordered your fears, explore your level of motivation to confront these fears by answering the following questions in your journal:

    - How real are these fears to me?
    - How much power in my life do these fears have?
    - How do these fears explain past or current actions in my life?
    - How do these fears determine my self-image, self-concept, and self-esteem?
    - How do these fears disable me?
    - How do these fears inhibit me?
    - What emotions do these fears block?
    - How long have I had these fears?
    - What have I done to overcome these fears?
    - How convinced am I of the need to confront these fears?

3. Once you have explored your motivation for confronting your fears, convince yourself of the need to address these fears. On a separate sheet of paper, answer these questions:
    - How do your fears influence your decision-making process?
    - How do your fears encourage and exacerbate your sense of insecurity?
    - How do your fears keep you from making a change in your life?
    - How do your fears influence your response to offers of help from others?
    - How have your fears kept you chained down and locked in?
    - How have your fears influenced your educational, career and work pursuits?
    - How have your fears contributed to your self-destructiveness?
    - How have your fears affected your belief in a healthy future for you?
    - How have your fears kept you from growing as a person?
    - How have your fears contributed to an unhealthy lifestyle for you?
4. Now that you are motivated to confront your fears, address the following issues in your journal (these issues need to be addressed before you can proceed to the fifth step):
    - What new behavior do I need to develop in order to confront my fears?
    - What beliefs block my desires and attempts at confronting my fears?

- How willing am I to try out new behaviors?
- How willing am I to use some of the tools available to overcome fears?
- What new beliefs do I need to confront my fears?

5. Once you are committed to confronting your fears, use tools found in this book to identify strategies in confronting each fear. For each of your fears, list the tools you can use to overcome it, referring to the Toolbox section in this book.

Task 4: Reinterpreting fear

It is human nature for many of our decisions to be motivated by the fear of pain. Perhaps the pain takes the form of feeling like a failure, hurt by rejection, or feeling inadequate.

From now on, I want you to think that the feeling of fear is just a signal. Perhaps the signal that fear is giving you is that there is something on the horizon that you need to prepare for. So, the new meaning that you are to attach to any feeling of fear is: "I feel fear and therefore preparation is required. I have the resources to break the issue down and prepare, prepare, prepare."

When I approach fear, I remind myself of the acronym, Forgetting Everything is All Right. It doesn't necessarily shift the fear, but it does allow me to confront it with a healthier mindset. I usually liken fear to driving a car—if it's in the driver's seat, with its hands firmly planted on the wheel, it's my job to move it to the passenger seat, the boot, or better still, leave it at the side of the road!

Hello Coach!

I remember that I used to get quite scared about job interviews when I was younger. That's a pretty relatable fear for a lot of people. What do you wear? What do you say? How can I relate to this person? You want to impress the person who has the power to promote you to your future or deny it. (I don't look at it this way anymore, but that's how I used to think about it and it was particularly fear-inducing.) Eventually I decided that there had to be a better way than suffering through this unnecessary agony and anxiety, so I ended up wrangling a friend into helping me video myself being interviewed for the job that I wanted. I practiced and reviewed, and although I couldn't know all the questions that I'd be asked, I'd at the very least have some sense of control over what I could bring to the interview and a stronger sense of confidence about how I could perform in the interview. I find preparation around any source of fear for me is really helpful.

I also like to look at fear from a worst-case scenario position: what could possibly go wrong? If we're looking at the job interview scenario, it's bombing out in the interview and not getting the job. If you end up not getting the job, it's not the end of the world, but it does present you with an opportunity to do better next time and find ways to improve. That could be through research and study about the people or business you're interviewing with, role playing, interning. Whatever it is, the whole point is to not let fear stand in your way of doing the things that are important to you.

You might also find it useful to talk through fearful circumstances with a coach, friend, or mentor to figure out what is the underlying reason for your fear. Is it real or is it what I call a non-truth? Are you going to let a non-truth dictate your life? No. So the key is to understand where the fear is coming from and with the right strategies, actions, and solutions, move beyond the fear to the life that you love.

When you expose your fears to the light of thoughtful examination, they usually evaporate and can be addressed by systematic action.

Practice asking yourself the following questions (you may wish to write down the answers):

What are the worst things that could happen?

1. _____

2. _____

3. _____

4. _____

5. _____

What are the best things that could happen?

1. _____

2. _____

3. _____

4. _____

5. _____

What's most likely to happen?

1. _____

2. _____

3. _____

4. _____

5. _____

The big question: What are you afraid to ask for?

I want you to make a list of completions for the following sentence: "When it comes to asking for what I want, I am afraid to …"

List ten things you are afraid to ask for:

1. _____
2. _____
3. _____
4. _____
5. _____
6. _____
7. _____
8. _____
9. _____
10. _____

The next step is to go back over each item in the preceding list and change the structure of the sentence to:

"I would really like to _____ *and I scare myself by imagining* _____ *"*

1. _____
2. _____
3. _____
4. _____
5. _____
6. _____
7. _____
8. _____
9. _____
10. _____

Can you see more clearly and specifically how you scare yourself? It is you who is making up all these negative scenarios that have not really happened. Your brain cannot tell the difference between a real event and a vividly imagined event, so you will actually feel scared—in some cases, even petrified—yet it can all be overcome by recognizing that fear can be reframed to be a healthy and challenging form of growth. However, the power that fear holds over each of us is nothing more than our minds running amok with unlikely and limiting scenarios. Once we have the tools to recognize and break down the fear that we are harboring, we have the power to move through it.

Your affirmation for facing your fears

"I am courageous, brave, and strong, and believe in myself."

Your daily must-do

"Mind chatter" dump time. Replace those negative thoughts with positive thoughts and have a wonderful day!

Self-esteem

Self-esteem is generally defined as self-worth, self-love, or self-satisfaction. It can be high, in some cases too high (narcissism), or low, reflected and played out in an undervaluing of self. Most people who are looking to effect change in their life through coaching have come to me with low self-esteem. It's been my experience that sometimes the best of us suffer from bouts of self-doubt that can leave us crippled. However, there are ways to work through these doubts and recognize them as opportunities to create change.

As you know from the beginning of this book, my discovery of coaching was brought about by having very low self-esteem. I was going through the motions at work, I was a new mother, I was in a very unhappy marriage, I hadn't come close to addressing my abuse, and I was literally running on fumes. I didn't think that I was doing a good job in any aspect of my life. I was a mess inside and out, and I had zero self-love.

I inherently believe that boosting your self-esteem doesn't need to take loads of time or exorbitant amounts of money. Building your self-esteem isn't about changing who you are—it's about embracing all of the positive aspects of you that have been cast aside for whatever reason. We all have strengths; that's the beautiful part of the human spirit. But true self-esteem means embracing all of our imperfections as well, and learning to recognize the beauty in these gifts.

The following tasks will not only boost your confidence, but they will also increase your energy levels and give you greater clarity of mind, plus provide a deeper knowledge of who you are. They will nourish your body, mind, and soul, and help you feel happier and more confident to step out of your shadow and into the light.

In the following tasks, there are suggested ways to create change and increase your confidence, working with the philosophy that long-lasting change starts on the inside. Let's take a look at the ways you can increase confidence by embracing your body, emotions, energy, mind, and spirit.

Task 5: Ten ways to boost your confidence

It may not be immediately obvious how the following ten actions and activities can boost your self-esteem but trust me, they will. The act of paying attention to yourself, of showing yourself regard and affection, is very powerful. You don't have to walk around saying "I am wonderful" in order to boost your self-esteem—and it won't work anyway if you don't really believe it! I have seen the following ten ways to boost confidence have a fantastic effect in my own life and the lives of others.

1. Vision

Write a script or vision of your ideal day or week in which you are feeling one hundred percent confident. If you're not clear on how great you will look and feel being assertive and confident, how will you create it? Start by thinking about how your new life will look and what will be different because you are feeling confident. Are you feeling self-conscious, shy, inferior, or just plain down? If you answered "yes", you're definitely not alone. Asking yourself these questions can help to set the scene:

- What do I look like when I'm feeling confident? Do I smile more? Do I appear happier?
- What does my body language say about me? Do I walk with my head high and shoulders back? Or do I walk with my head looking down?
- What clothes do I wear? Do I wear clothes that reflect the fact that I feel great? Or do I wear clothes that camouflage my true self?
- How would I talk to colleagues and family while feeling confident?
- What type of relationships would I choose to have if I was feeling confident? Would these types of relationships support and nourish me? Do I feel good around these people?
- What nurturing activities would I choose to do while feeling good about myself?

Here's a short example that may help you with this exercise.

I have woken up and put on my favorite pair of jeans that fit in all the right places and make me look and feel like the strong, healthy person I am. I've done my hair and make-up and it reflects how I feel on the inside, which is great! I really have this day locked in and it's all going my way. I'm headed into a meeting with a new client for which I've prepared well, and I am looking forward to displaying how researched I am and how I will be the best person to take on this account. In fact, I'm feeling so grounded in my own confidence this morning that I'm going to stop by my neighborhood coffee shop on the way and shout myself a latte.

2. Write a happy list

This is a simple exercise that's very powerful. Try writing a list of everything that makes you happy—this could be anything from walking on the beach to having a long bath. Then, at the beginning of each week, schedule at least one of these experiences in your diary every day. Allocate a specific time for it to ensure you'll make it happen. With this simple system, your life soon becomes filled with many more enjoyable, happy moments. The more you focus on being happy, the more it will happen.

Things that make me happy:

1. _____

2. _____

3. _____

4. _____

5. _____

3. Trust yourself

Do you doubt yourself too often? Do you trust what other people have to say and act upon their opinions instead of trusting yourself? Listen to what your heart says and not what others think you should do or say. When you listen to what you want, it creates an immense sense of self-confidence, and putting your feelings and thoughts into action is more powerful. If you don't listen and trust yourself, who will?

Start by trusting one decision each day and watch how this simple exercise can increase your self-esteem. Watch how others' opinions reflect your own; if others mistrust your judgment or opinions, it could just be a mirror of what you truly feel about yourself.

Practice "inner knowing"—knowing what will happen that day for you. In the morning, write a list of what you think will happen based on your intuition, then watch what unfolds.

4. Stepping out of your shadow

During this process of finding your confidence and self-esteem, take some quiet time and use your journal to review your past and present circumstances, looking for clues as to why you have created repeated scenarios in your life that have kept you in your shadow and prevented you from shining.

Complete the following statements:

The people I stand in the shadow of are:

    1. _____

    2. _____

3. _____

4. _____

5. _____

The reason for this is:

_____

I stand in my own shadow because I fear:

_____

The times I have shone my light and felt at my best were:

_____

The one action I'll take to step out of my shadow is:

_____

The people I admire are:

1. _____

2. _____

3. _____

4. _____

5. _____

I admire them because:

1. _____
2. _____
3. _____
4. _____
5. _____

What steps can I take to surround myself with these people more?

1. _____
2. _____
3. _____
4. _____
5. _____

5. Food

Think about what you eat. Food can lift your energy levels and make you feel good; it can also have the opposite effect. If you eat too many processed foods—white sugar, potato chips, etc.—you may get a quick energy boost, but you will feel tired shortly after. You may even get headaches and stomach cramps, and in the long term, this can sometimes lead to depression, among other illnesses.

Check in with yourself to see if the things you eat and drink are suitable for your body:

Do you drink alcohol or smoke?

Do you consume more than two liters of water each day to replenish your body?

Do you eat enough fruit and vegetables?

What five things can I change in my diet?

1. _____
2. _____
3. _____
4. _____
5. _____

6. Energy

Which activities in your life boost your energy levels? What exercise do you do each day? Which people or friends boost your energy? Which people or situations drain your energy? How can you avoid putting yourself in these situations? Can you say "no" more often?

List five things that will increase your energy:

1. _____
2. _____

3. _____

4. _____

5. _____

7. Play

How much fun do you experience each day? Do you laugh every single day? Here are some ideas to introduce fun and laughter in your life and have a giggle:

- Swing on a swing or slide down a slide at the neighborhood park.
- Eat an ice cream.
- Cuddle a baby, a kitten, or a puppy.
- Watch a funny video.
- Go to the beach.
- Go ice skating.
- Hang out with your friends.

List five ways you can have fun:

1. _____

2. _____

3. _____

4. _____

5. _____

Commit to focusing on new "fun" things each week and change what isn't working for you.

8. Express your love

In the hustle and bustle of our busy lives, it's easy to forget to take the time to show our love for those we care about. Ask yourself, "Who are the five people in the world I care the most about, and when was the last time I told them?"

It's also important to express love for yourself. How often do you tell yourself you are fabulous, clever, or beautiful? How often do you take time out to nurture yourself and take responsibility for your own self-love?

When we start to really love who we are on the inside, often the world reflects this back to us effortlessly. Conversely, when we have built our self-worth and self-love—or lack thereof— on the foundation of others' opinions of us, we often find that these opinions hold no real truth of who we are or how we feel. We have let ourselves believe falsehoods and half-truths about ourselves because someone else said so, whether from a place of kindness or not. The point is that we have to love who we are based on what we internally perceive and measure that to be, not what someone else tells us. External validation, as we have previously explored, is not self-sustaining; it's temporary and sometimes has no basis in reality at all.

You are an amazing person who has many gifts to give; however, if you don't recognize them, who else will? Start by loving and nourishing yourself without relying on others to do it for you.

Suggestions for self-love:

- Tell others how much you love them.
- Have an aromatherapy bath.

- Pamper yourself with a massage.
- Paint your toenails pink.
- Put a facial mask on at home.
- Walk in the rain.
- Watch a sunrise or sunset and write about how it makes you feel.
- Dance at home when no one is watching.
- Sing like no one is listening.
- Let people close to you know how you like to be loved.

9. Take a risk

Do something that pushes you out of your comfort zone, such as joining a drama, dance, or art class, and stretch your mind and body into unfamiliar territory. Acknowledge your effort in doing this. How great will you feel once you have done something new that challenged you?

List five new things you would like to try:

1. _____
2. _____
3. _____
4. _____
5. _____

10. Affirmations

Each night for thirty nights, before you go to bed, write down an affirmation or say it mentally. It has been proven that saying or writing mantras or affirmations increases your chances of creating that intention in your life. Give it a try and see what happens.

The five things I will focus on this week are:

1. _____
2. _____
3. _____
4. _____
5. _____

Your affirmation for boosting your self-esteem

"I am confident, and I love life."

Your daily must-do

As each new day begins, so too does the chance to increase our mental capacity for positivity. Every time we approach the "mind chatter" dump, we are letting go of negative thoughts and creating space for positive ones. Every. Single. Time.

Your review

1. What were my personal highlights during this emotional phase?
2. What challenges did I face and how did I handle them?
3. What exciting new insights did I discover about myself?

4. What was my greatest achievement in this phase?
5. What is my commitment for the next phase?

Remember

By the end of this book, you will discover what inspires you and who you want to be—and then you'll achieve it.

Your checklist

A. Complete Task 1: Working through the years.
B. Complete Task 2: Patterns.
C. Complete Task 3: Overcoming fear.
D. Complete Task 4: Reinterpreting fear.
E. Complete Task 5: Ten ways to boost your confidence.
F. Write out affirmations and verbalize daily.
G. Daily must-do: "mind chatter" dump.
H. Complete review.

CHECKING IN AGAIN

Before you move on to the next chapter, which deals with your energetic self, now is a good time to review your roadblocks, the Manifestation Tool, and affirmations.

Roadblock exercise

For the full Roadblock exercise, go back and refresh your memory of it if you need to and repeat the practical tips on how to complete it if you'd like to do it again as a refresher.

The Manifestation Tool

Is the following equation still at the front of your mind?

My purpose + thoughts + vision + my words + feelings + actions + gratitude = goal.

Affirmations

Also review the affirmations you have been working with. If you need to adjust them to reflect the changes you have already gone through, refer back to the Affirmations chapter.

Visualizations

If you haven't practiced visualizing the movie of your life recently, it's time to try it again. You may find that the movie has changed since the last time you "played" it—observe the changes but don't try to explain them to yourself, and certainly don't make any judgments about what's changed.

SPIRIT

All of your work in the last four dimensions—body, energy, thoughts, and feelings—was designed to bring you to this fifth dimension, spirit, in good shape, ready to move into a brilliant new place in your life. There is still some work to do in this section, but by now you should be starting to feel the "flow" of what you're doing.

By this stage in the process of change, doing the tasks set for you in each chapter should not be too difficult to face and you should no longer feel confronted by what you are discovering. Rather, you should feel invigorated by the energy shift from within and the growth in self-awareness. Indeed, you might be feeling exuberant about the life that is unfolding right now and wanting to forge ahead with clarity, connection, and oneness. In this chapter, we will explore the concept of spirituality in your life.

I have strong views about spirituality, both personally and professionally. I also have strong views about what is right for me as a functioning, compassionate human being. I also want to state very clearly that I make no judgment about what spirituality means to another person. It's personal; however, I do believe that it should be supportive, positive, comforting, and uplifting.

I've also found in my professional experience with coaching that there is often misunderstanding around the use of certain words and techniques to do with the spiritual realm, so I'd like to take a little time here to just clarify what all these terms mean to me and to establish those meanings clearly since they underpin so much of the work that you have been doing thus far.

My personal definition of spirituality is anything that transcends the physical or material world. I refer to this as our soul or spirit. It's all the good stuff that is in essence utter joy and deep connectivity with self—emotional, mental, and quite often elemental. This is more than just energetic as it takes all the dimensions equally and joins them as one. It quite often appears to me that there is confusion between what is meant by spirituality and religion as people tend to use the words interchangeably. For clarification, I am not talking about religion, Christianity, or any type of formal religious practice when I speak of spirituality, but rather acknowledging the deeper sense of self and the ability to connect with a higher being, whatever you perceive that to be. I was raised Catholic, but I have moved away from the formal practice of Catholicism over the years. My position is that we have many different labels for God and spirituality, and we need to focus on what works for us as individuals.

While we're on the subject, I want to take the time to delve into the meanings of mindfulness, meditation, and prayer, as they pertain to my coaching and beliefs in general.

Mindfulness is simply the practice of being aware and fully awake in the present moment, not concentrating on the past or the future, and living without judgment or opinion, just merely being. It's a muscle that we need to exercise constantly because as a society we have been conditioned to think, opine, and judge based on history and/or projection into the future. We're never encouraged to think in the stillness of the present moment. In fact, we're raised to live in a space of holding tension. This can be limiting, fearful and just plain exhausting. If we were lifted up in our thinking as children to pause and live without expectation, just be in the joy of the moment, we would in all likelihood find ourselves dropping limiting thought patterns as we mature into adulthood.

Meditation is a technique that I have practiced on and off over the years. It was something that I was exposed to as a child. My mother would often have her "quiet time"—twenty minutes in the morning and evening—and I witnessed the calming effect that it had on her. As I grew into a teenager, I was encouraged to practice this as well. These days, meditation is part of my daily practice as it helps me to not only become more mindful but also place myself in a position of connection with soul or spirit. Meditation, in its more common reference, is used as a tool to promote stress reduction and mindfulness. I find it useful for taking a beat and giving myself the space to work through any issues that I'm having trouble with.

For me, prayer is a mindfulness technique that allows me quiet time to connect with my faith and source, soul, The Universe, The Divine, God, Creator or higher self, whatever you choose to call your soul or spirit guides. I find that prayer allows me to practice gratitude and seek solutions and guidance when I'm challenged. The rewards from allowing this process into my life have brought a great deal of enhancement to my achievements. I spend time in meditation and prayer each day and it fuels my soul. It's the place where I give thanks and request guidance when answers aren't as apparent as I would like them to be. In my case, God often shows up with signs when I'm open and mindful.

To be a spiritual person, you really have to have your physical world locked down. It's that simple. The dimension of the body, energy, thoughts, and feelings need to have been worked through and brought into alignment so that you can flow into your spirituality. These aspects of yourself are all interconnected and rely heavily on each other to work at their peak. Once you're operating at your peak, you'll be attuned to the laws of the universe and you'll start attracting your desires like a giant magnet. Fully clear and open, you'll be manifesting at your highest level.

Self-love

Developing self-love

For many people, self-love may be the greatest and most important love they ever experience in this lifetime. However, "learning to love yourself" may not seem so easy to achieve. For most of us, genuine self-love seems so elusive and so much harder to grasp than we expected. I often talk about the importance of self-love. Now I would like to give you some practical suggestions—some first steps—on how to begin to learn to love yourself.

I often use the analogy that if you keep giving to others without giving to yourself, it is like pouring water from a vessel. If you pour and pour without ever refilling it, eventually it will run dry. So if you are like that vessel, how do you refill, recharge, re-energize, and replenish yourself so that you will have energy and love to give to others and to the world? The answer is to love and give to yourself first.

How can you begin to do this? The following tasks should help.

Task 1: Caring for yourself

There are many ways for you to love and to care for yourself; the possibilities are infinite. The following list contains several suggestions. Not all of them may appeal to you—just try to work with as many as possible.

- Review the areas of your life where you feel there is a lack of love.
- Continually review your belief systems about receiving love and practice the tools to shift these beliefs.
- Eat healthy foods and exercise regularly.
- Treat yourself to a massage, a facial, a pedicure, or a gym membership.
- Take a bubble bath, eat dinner at home by candlelight, take a walk on the beach, swim in the ocean (those waters are very healing), or watch a sunset.
- Whether alone, with a friend, or a partner, have a night out on the town. Go out for a nice dinner, go dancing, attend the theater, a concert, the ballet, or a movie.
- If you tend to be a workaholic—or if you are more a saver than a spender— perhaps it is time to take a well-deserved, long-overdue holiday.
- Take time to paint or to write.

Doing something that you get pleasure from, without guilt or judgment attached to it, is showing yourself care. For a lot of us, taking personal time to participate in an activity that we love can be attached to feelings of guilt, or a sense that we should be doing something more useful with our time. These limiting beliefs may have taken a lifetime to develop, so it makes sense that they're going to take a while to undo, but have faith that you can step away from feelings of guilt or shame when you're taking time out for yourself and know that, in short order, you'll no longer feel anything but joy when you nurture yourself.

Task 2: Learning to love yourself

What are five ways I can learn to love myself?

1. _____
2. _____
3. _____
4. _____
5. _____

Task 3: Self-talk

Another way to enhance self-love and self-esteem is to be aware of your self-talk (those things that you say to yourself inside your head). Speak to yourself in ways that are more kind and less demeaning or abusive. Many of us have very harsh inner critics. When we make a mistake, this critical voice inside our head beats up on us, saying things like, "That was so stupid!" or "I can't do anything right!" or "What a loser!"

It's imperative that you replace these negative messages with other, more positive ones. For example, "I made a mistake. That's okay.

That is how I learn. I'll know better next time." With awareness, over time you can catch yourself when your self-talk is negative and change the message to something more positive and ego-enhancing.

Make sure you don't just catch yourself "being wrong"; catch yourself being right. In other words, don't just catch the voice of your inner critic and stop it from beating up on you. When you do something well, or when you find yourself saying the right things to yourself or to others, be sure to reward yourself; acknowledge yourself verbally, give yourself a pat on the back, or treat yourself to something special.

What self-talk can you begin to say to yourself that will reaffirm that you love you?

1. _____
2. _____
3. _____
4. _____
5. _____

Task 4: Defining love

Write down the answers to the following in your notebook or journal.

What is love to you?

1. _____

2. _____

3. _____

4. _____

5. _____

How do you measure love?

1. _____

2. _____

3. _____

4. _____

5. _____

How do you love yourself and the people in your life?

1. _____

2. _____

3. _____

4. _____

5. _____

How does love look in your life?

1. _____

2. _____

3. _____

4. _____

5. _____

Do you know how to self-love? How do you self-love?

1. _____

2. _____

3. _____

4. _____

5. _____

Do you socialize with people who "do love" (that is, "express love") your way—have you ever told them what love is to you?

_____

Time out for you—what can you do for fifteen minutes each day to show yourself self-love?

1. _____

2. _____

3. _____

4. _____

5. _____

Your affirmation for self-love

"I truly love and accept myself."

Your daily must-do

By now you know what to do. Practice with kindness, compassion, and self-love your daily negative "mind chatter" dump and be prepared for those loving positive thoughts to flow to you.

Forgiveness

Finding forgiveness

Life will always bring us opportunities to grow. The more we resist these opportunities, the greater the frustration we feel within ourselves and in our daily lives. If we experience conflict, or if we've had traumatic situations in our lives that have resulted in feelings of anger, hurt, and sadness, it can be easy to blame the people who we believe have hurt us, or the situations themselves, for making us feel that we have been wronged. We project blame, criticism, and judgment as a way to avoid dealing with our own feelings and, most times, efforts to forgive ourselves and others. Criticizing, blaming, and judging others is no way to create transformation. In fact, it is a roadblock to the creation of change. And as I've said throughout this book, and I say to my clients when they reach a block, avoiding it is not going to fix it. We must pause, confront, examine, learn, and remedy the roadblock; otherwise, we will be stuck on the same hamster wheel for the foreseeable future.

Any situation that raises negative emotions within us presents us with the opportunity to learn. Rather than latching onto blame, criticism, and judgment when we are in pain, we need to embrace the lesson that is being presented to us from this clearly unresolved and painful position. Most of the time, we're just trying to avoid the pain we're in by projecting all those negative feelings onto someone else. It relieves us of the responsibility of dealing with the pain temporarily but it doesn't heal us in the long term, and hence our roadblock remains in the same immovable state that it has always been. But there is a way forward.

Finding forgiveness within is one of the greatest lessons and gifts that you will experience in your lifetime. It doesn't have to be a big issue, although you can certainly tackle the big issues, but you can start small and progress once you feel the benefit of finding forgiveness working in your life.

People will upset and disappoint you—it's a guarantee. You will upset and disappoint yourself—that's also a guarantee. But knowing this also allows you to understand that you can work toward forgiveness and a brighter future.

Sometimes the hurt is a little thing. A boss at work annoys you with their dismissive manner of address, friend flakes on you at the last minute time after time, your kids tear up the house at the worst possible moment. All of these minor irritations can be forgiven relatively easily if you're willing to pause, take a step away from the situation, realize what is going on for the other person involved, and understand how that behavior triggers you. Practicing forgiveness for yourself and others in these less significant circumstances flexes your forgiveness muscle when you're presented with bigger difficulties that really seem overwhelming.

I want to tell you about a friend of mine. Her marriage hadn't been working for a long time and the end was inevitable but necessary. While she was married, my friend had built up a business that meant a great deal to her but that had little to do with her ex; however, through some complications, he ended up with it. Obviously, it took a toll on my friend and she grieved the end of her marriage and the loss of her business for a long time. Those were big issues that she had to work through, but she did because she knew she wanted more out of life. She felt that life had more to offer her, and she had more to offer life.

Regardless of the hurt that surrounded her, she knew that one day, with persistence and practicality, she'd be in a better place. But in order for her to be able to move forward, she had to find a place that she could park all the negativity around what happened to her and focus on the good that was and would be in her life.

Getting to her point of forgiveness didn't happen overnight. She did, however, make a point of practicing forgiveness for herself and her ex every day until the whole situation just became easier and her sense of self came together with the rest of her dimensions.

Forgiving herself for the end of the marriage was the first thing that she learned she needed to do to be able to move forward. Berating herself as some sort of failure for not staying in a situation that was clearly not working was clouding her ability to think about the future with clarity, hope, and purpose—key ingredients in creating change.

Once my friend was able to forgive herself, she began to experience a stronger ability to be able to practice forgiveness toward her former partner. She was able to clearly see the place of fear and anxiety that he was operating from and she was able to respond calmly to his demands, in turn strengthening her ability to believe in herself and her new path forward. None of it came without work, but these days she is able to see all the gains that came from the relationship, the personal growth, wisdom, and even day-to-day coping skills that she acquired while going through the divorce. When she's presented with issues—major or minor in her life—she's able to look at them with a bit more serenity and a desire to find the best possible outcome for herself and those around her without resorting to anger in the first instance.

The gift of forgiveness

We can spend so much time feeling hurt or badly done by that we become caught up in the drama and we lose sight of the gift or lesson that is presented to us. Sometimes this lesson is about the other person; more often than not, though, the learning involves us on some level. Finding forgiveness calls for us to challenge and change our perceptions about a current situation and there is no doubt that this can be one of the more difficult areas for us to create change in. It's uncomfortable and requires a great deal of acceptance, calm, and serenity.

If you can take time to create forgiveness in your world, it will free up your energy and also assist you to heal and learn at a faster rate. While you harbor resentment or anger, you are crippling your healing. The best way of truly being free to create what you desire in life is to resolve your emotional grief.

Allowing for the gift of forgiveness is a choice that we can make. Sometimes, that choice needs to be made daily; sometimes it's a one-and-done situation. More often than not, it's every iteration in between those two extremes. None of it is wrong, or lazy, or too high-minded. It's just whatever works for you. What is important is that we allow forgiveness to be part of our lives. It's one of the most beautiful aspects of being a sensitive and caring human, being able to let forgiveness lead us, and also being able to be forgiven.

Being able to place yourself in the space of forgiveness is truly a gift that we give ourselves. While we may not forget the hurts or injustices that have crossed our paths, our hearts, minds, and souls benefit greatly from the act of forgiveness. It means putting a framework around acts that have been perpetrated against us—either by ourselves or others—that no longer serve us, and letting them go. It might not happen immediately, but with dedication to the desire to be on the other side of those grievances, a state of grace can be achieved.

Emotional intelligence is loosely defined as having the ability to understand and manage your emotions. When we speak about forgiveness, we are indeed connecting with our emotions to gain insight and understanding into the art of forgiveness, because being able to forgive, to a certain degree means being able to harness our emotions and direct them in a certain way, leading to a certain outcome. Having strong emotional intelligence is a wonderful attribute, but developing it is an exercise that few of us spend enough time on. Admittedly, it has taken society quite some time to learn to value our emotions in the same way that we value intelligence and material possessions. However, now is the time to really harness your emotional self and understand and value what it adds to your life. As your awareness around your emotional self grows, you will see the impact it has on your life and relationships, how you relate to others and yourself.

Being honest

It is critical to look at your own issues and be honest with yourself about what you still don't forgive yourself for. Learning to access forgiveness takes courage and patience and truthfulness. It matters that we own our truth and advocate for ourselves. Even if the words that we use to encapsulate our truth are not perfect, it is the principle behind the acknowledgment that is important. Speaking up for ourselves and our beliefs is critical to self-empowerment.

Sometimes we have to learn how to be honest and often this can start with accessing our truth—the stuff we really think. You need to connect with your opinions, thoughts, and judgments. Start listening to yourself, to your inner voice, your thoughts, your body, and your spirit.

Getting to the heart of the matter is often one of the most difficult tasks you will face—however, it's a valuable and worthwhile undertaking.

Honoring our truth is a splendid feeling and a beautiful gift—are you giving yourself this gift? Be aware that you do not always have to speak your truth. Your mind is so powerful that sometimes you will want to shut out the truth; your fears may be so great that you will be scared to face them. You may also be so scared of the change that may result from facing your truth that you'd rather just stay numb. But by actually facing the truth of how you feel or the situation that you find yourself in, you may not need to do another thing. You may not have to express anything or confront anyone—and confrontation is often one of our biggest fears. Ideally, you will start to feel your truth, experience it, and know it within you, and then decide when it is right for you to speak up about it.

For example, you have a controlling and overpowering friend and whenever you spend time together, you feel angry and pushed around by her behavior. You may also feel helpless that you are being abused, walked over, and not respected.

Instead, look at this as an opportunity for growth and think about these questions: What am I making that person "wrong" for? Why am I judging them? What is this person teaching me to do or be? What do I have to stand for in my life? Could it be, perhaps, that this friend reminds me of a parent or employer who pushed me around and to whom I didn't say anything?

Instead of internalizing the anger or frustration you feel when you are around this person, express it. Tell them how you feel and set up new rules in the relationship about what is acceptable to you. Realize that your friend's behavior is a mirror of what they have learned and could be a way of covering up their own fear of being out of control, which is why they boss people around. The gift of learning from your experience with your friend could be that you speak up and say no to anyone who acts this way toward you and tell them how you feel about their behavior.

Living forgiveness

Do you know how to courageously ask for what you want? Are you able to tell someone you love how unhappy you are? Can you tell someone you are hurting?

One of the best things you can do is face the truth of your own feelings and start acknowledging your truth. Then you will live in alignment with what you value, and you will also feel comfortable facing the not-so-pretty parts of who you are—and you can then start to embrace these parts instead of vilifying them.

Forgiveness and acceptance cannot happen when you do not face the truth of yourself in a situation and continually blame others for what is happening. If you take responsibility, respond to yourself, see your contribution, and feel this, you will find that the issue will unravel itself at an unconscious and conscious level and you will find a place of acceptance.

Over my years of coaching, I've pretty much seen it all and there's not much that surprises me anymore, but there are some issues that arise over and over again that clients ask my advice about. One of these topics is self-acceptance for some of the messier aspects of our lives. A lot of times, we feel slighted by people and situations and we want to lash out as a means of self-protection and push the blame for our behavior onto others, accepting little or no responsibility for our own imperfect actions.

A lesson that I needed to learn around taking personal responsibility was around my divorce. Regardless of the fact that things were not as they should be and it was a very unhealthy environment for me and my child to be in, I had to face up to the fact that I had agreed to marry this person in the first place and I had participated in enabling some behavior that I knew, even as I was doing it, was detrimental to my wellbeing. I felt shame, guilt, and complicity around my acts, my own misguided thoughts about being such a great person that I could rescue this man from his demons, and the fact that I had failed at marriage.

With a lot of work and self-reflection, I was able to accept my role in the end of my marriage and examine the aspects of its end that were lessons for me. Even though the marriage didn't work out, I was able to walk away from that relationship knowing myself better and my own personal relationship boundaries. I was also able to be grateful for the marriage, as without it I would never have been able to be a mother to such a beautiful son. The pain that I endured actually gave me the gift of wisdom to understand that I had lessons to learn and there was nothing fruitless about the relationship, because it ultimately taught me so much that has enhanced my life after it.

Task 5: Asking for forgiveness

Are you "doing" forgiveness in your life? List who with, and in what areas of your life, you want to find forgiveness. Where is it non-existent? Decide what you are willing to commit to doing about it.

Your options could be to write a forgiveness letter or email and send it on, write it down on paper and have a goodbye burning ceremony—a forgiveness party—with lots of candles, or verbally express your forgiveness for certain people and/or situations.

Task 6: Visualization

One way you can forgive is through visualization. With your eyes closed, visualize all the people in your life whom you would like to forgive. Once you have them staring at you, standing in front of you, one by one say hello, tell them you forgive them and send them off to be free with love. Set yourself free and those you love. Practice this before you go to sleep at night over a seven-night period.

Your affirmation for forgiveness

"I unconditionally love and accept myself."

Your daily must-do

Understanding and practicing forgiveness may have raised some extra negative thoughts, so pay attention to your "mind chatter" dump at this time and be kind to yourself. This is part of practicing forgiveness.

Gratitude: The human magnet

Gratitude can be thought of as appreciation, or the act of being thankful; essentially, the old-fashioned notion of counting your blessings. It's an emotion, and like many emotions, it sometimes needs a little daily practice to remain in peak condition. When we "practice" gratitude, like mindfulness, meditation, or prayer, the "muscle" of gratitude gets stronger, and as a result, we become more resilient, grounded, and happier human beings.

It extends that if we think of ourselves as a giant magnet, whatever we are feeling—love, anger, fear, happiness, joy, resistance, or gratitude—we are in essence creating a magnetic force that will attract those feelings or energies directly to us. Fear of something creates a magnetic force that will attract more of what you fear. Expressing gratitude for something projects a magnetic force that attracts more of what you're grateful for.

At any time that you are not expressing gratitude for an outcome, you are basically resisting the outcome; thus, your focus is on not wanting that outcome. That means your thoughts and emotions are fixated on not wanting the outcome. That focus of not wanting only serves to draw to you more of what you're not wanting, more of what you're resisting.

There is no doubt that this is very much an easier-said-than-done exercise, but there is nothing more gratifying than seeing abundance being returned to you. Gratefulness begets gratefulness. However, like anything worthwhile, it doesn't just happen by willing it into existence. One has to actually sincerely practice this.

As part of my daily ritual, I lie in bed each morning and mentally go through a list of people, situations, experiences, stuff that I'm grateful for. Sometimes it's a thirty-second exercise. I think of my son, my dog, my home, health, those sorts of things. At other times, I'm really focused on one person or situation completely, like a meeting that I just had that moved some plans forward, or an old client that may have reached out and given me an update about their life. It can even be a new skill that I learned, or even some information that I picked up from a podcast that really made my day. Whatever it is, the acknowledgment of gratitude around that person or situation grounds me and makes my heart swell with love and joy. I find just performing this simple act puts a smile on my face (sometimes when I'm not even in the mood to smile) and helps point me in the right direction for the day.

I also take a moment to say thank you and practice gratitude at the end of my day. Again, that small action brings me joy and peace and reminds me that the good fortune I have in my life has been hard-earned and is well-deserved.

The power of you

Since your current outcomes are based on what you have thought and felt at some point in the past, and those outcomes are now being experienced in your life, guess who created them? You did! And although that may not make you feel any better about them just yet, consider this: since it is you who is responsible for attracting and creating "undesirable outcomes", it is also you who is responsible for attracting and creating "desirable outcomes"! And that is a wonderfully powerful space to live in.

When you recognize the fact that you brought these outcomes into your life, you will gain an understanding of your creative power. This should, in turn, instill in you a sense of gratitude that you can choose what you will create for your life. Prior to understanding how this process works, you were "unconsciously creating"; now you can begin to "consciously create" a life for which you can be even more grateful. This is very much like harnessing a gift that you had no control over, and the more that you start to exert focus and control over the conscious creation of your life, the greater the rewards.

If you perceive that something is going wrong in your life, it's only your perception based on a lack of understanding that everything unfolds in your life perfectly, just as you choose and instruct. In the bigger scheme of things, nothing ever goes "wrong." The process of creation never wavers. It is, has been, and always will be perfect, precise, and unfailing one hundred percent of the time.

When I'm focused on creating favorable outcomes in my own life, I start with my morning ritual of gratitude, prayer, meditation, and the setting of the intention for the day. It could be something really simple like wanting to feel calm and present throughout the day. To do this, I'll set an intention around calm and presence, and combine those thoughts with visualization techniques. I'll look at my diary and literally visualize an image of me feeling calm and present during all the activities during the day. I'll remain mindful of my intention, so that when I'm in my meetings, or even just driving to them, if I feel triggered by someone saying something unkind or another driver cutting me off, I'll remember to bring my thinking back around to calm and present. I might find a place to park or sit at my desk for a moment, and just practice some deep breathing and focus on bringing myself back to a state of calmness and presence in the moment. These are techniques that I find useful for calming my own nerves and creating favorable outcomes. Obviously, there are many other ways that will work for people and it's important to work out what is going to be beneficial to you.

The miracle of creation

It's important to recognize and express gratitude for the fact that everything in your life is a miracle that you have created. Creation, regardless of how you might perceive it, is always a miracle. If you can learn to express gratitude for every miracle in your life, you will begin to see the life-changing power that gratitude holds in creating much more to be grateful for.

The miracles (creations) which show up that aren't in harmony with your intended or desired outcomes are merely signals that you need to make adjustments within yourself. When you fully grasp and internalize this truth, you'll learn to express gratitude for the signal that you actually created, and that you have been provided with the evidence that will enable you to change the thoughts, emotions, and perceptions which brought the outcome into your life.

Your perceptions regarding any event, condition, or circumstance are only based on a memory of something in the past that is stored in your unconscious mind and can be consciously changed if you discover that it is not in harmony with what you desire to accomplish.

When I'm thinking about the miracle of creation in my own life, my thinking immediately goes to my son. Around the time of his birth, I was exploring coaching and trying to really ascertain who I was and what I wanted to be in my life. I'd been struggling with the notion of unconditional love and feelings of not being worthy of such love since childhood, and here I was with a brand-new baby and overwhelming feelings of unconditional love for this child and, of course, he for me.

One situation, two perceptions

Let's look at two versions of the same situation and see firsthand what an attitude of gratitude is—and isn't.

Let's say that you wake up on a Saturday morning after a good night's rest. You've worked hard all week and you're really looking forward to getting outside and playing in a tennis tournament that you've entered and enjoying your weekend of rest and recreation.

You're feeling pretty good about the day ahead of you. You make your coffee, open the blinds, and look out the window. Argh—it's raining outside!

Next, your self-talk kicks in: "My whole day is ruined. I was planning on doing this and that, and now I can't. Why do things always have to happen like that? Another weekend ruined! I can't ever get a break."

Obviously, your perception is that everything went wrong and your whole weekend is ruined. Based on your thought pattern and perception, you're right: it is. Unless you are able to change that perception, you'll allow yourself to have a less than desirable weekend. In fact, by remaining in this state, you will literally attract additional events, conditions, and circumstances to you that will make certain that you have a less than desirable weekend.

This is a classic case of resistance or ingratitude. It's an example of refusing to see a silver lining.

Now let's take a look at the neighbor down the street who always seems to have things going her way. Let's imagine it's the same scenario: she has worked all week and made plans to play in the same tennis tournament that you were entered in.

She walks to the window, opens the shades, and sees exactly the same situation that you did when you opened them. Initially, she is a little disappointed because she can't go to the tennis tournament she was planning on, but there is nothing she can do to change the situation. She begins her habitual thought process and self-talk, which goes something like this: "I was certainly looking forward to that tennis tournament. Oh well, there are a few things that need to get done around here today anyway. That means I don't have to water the grass for a few days and that will save a little on my water bill. It's been a few weeks since it rained and we definitely needed it."

Although your neighbor was disappointed initially, she made a conscious decision not to allow the changed circumstance to ruin the entire weekend and shifted the focus to something more positive and productive. She made a space in her thought processes for gratitude.

Practicing gratitude doesn't happen overnight. Initially, finding that silver lining in difficult or less than optimal situations can be hard to do, but you've already been practicing an "attitude of gratitude" without even realizing. The daily "mind chatter" dump has been your jumping off point for letting go of negative thoughts and allowing space for positivity. Well, it doesn't get more positive than gratitude!

A state of gratitude

When you have developed a crystal clear understanding that all things work for the greater good no matter how bad things may appear, it becomes much easier to stay in a state of gratitude.

When you are able to fully develop that awareness (and with a little practice, you will), not only is it an extremely liberating experience but also you are setting yourself up for a much greater flow of abundance and happiness to come into every area of your life. When The Universe sees that you are grateful for what you have, it will send you more.

This is exactly how Universal Laws operate. The Universe doesn't perceive anything as good or bad; it only sends outcomes to you based on your energy vibration, and your attitude concerning any given thing is exactly what determines that vibrational resonance.

God, Universal Consciousness, or whatever you perceive it to be, loves each person unconditionally at the exact same level and delivers to each of us precisely what we are asking for, based on our individually chosen vibrational output. If your output is anger, fear, doubt, or worry, The Universe perceives that you are asking for outcomes based on that energy, and that is exactly what you'll receive. The same is true for your thoughts, which have an energetic and vibrational frequency that radiates a powerful force, like moths to a flame.

You can't possibly control everything that is going on around you in the world, but you can most certainly control yourself and how you perceive what's going on. And while it takes some training, concentration, and effort to shift your thinking and perception, it's worth every moment to do so.

Task 7: The Gratitude Game

I invite you to play the "Gratitude Game." The aim is to find creative and inexpensive ways to thank those people who often get overlooked. For example, you might acknowledge or appreciate those people that provide you with a service each day: the garage attendant, local grocery man, your mom or dad for helping you out, or a special friend who always supports you.

Get creative this week with your acknowledgments and notice the feeling you receive when you appreciate someone in your life who has helped you.

Task 8: An attitude of gratitude

Developing an attitude of gratitude is one of the most important things that you can do for attracting and manifesting the things that you desire into your life. In fact, if you have a desire to consistently attract opportune outcomes, it's essential that you cultivate this attitude. The following method is equally as effective and actually accomplishes the same end result as that contained in the first task.

Make a commitment to do the following for the next thirty days. Take out a piece of paper and each night make a handwritten list of the things you can think of that you are grateful for. Think deeply about each area of your life and begin to write in detail the good things that come to your mind as you write.

Don't fight it or strain in the attempt to come up with things; just allow them to flow. Depending on your particular situation, you may find that it's hard to come up with things to be grateful for initially, but dig deep and things will begin to flow. Make sure, though, that you are finding and writing things that you are sincerely grateful for.

If the emotion isn't there, the result won't be either. Let's say that you are working on a relationship issue. You and your significant other have been at odds for some time, and you are feeling really hurt and angry over the situation. Although your state of mind is telling you how angry you are, think about the good you saw in this person that attracted you to them initially. Begin to write down what comes to mind and more will follow. Write in as much detail as you are able regarding each item on your list. If it is hard initially, that's okay; just do the best you can. It will become easier the more you practice it.

For example, *I'm grateful for this person because:*

1. _____
2. _____
3. _____
4. _____
5. _____

Use this technique in whatever area of your life you are working on, whether it's money, health, relationships, or all three. It is extremely powerful, and with practice and persistence you will begin to see circumstances change almost magically.

Make a commitment to yourself that you will do this exercise at least once per day and stick to that commitment. It doesn't have to take a long time—even five minutes is better than none at all. Just make sure you do it every day.

Task 9: Practicing gratitude

Gratitude plays an extremely important role in beginning to consciously and intentionally create desired outcomes in your life. It's my hope that you'll think about this and choose gratitude as an attitude for yourself. It will make all the difference.

Make a list of all the people you would like to thank, and send a note or pick up the phone to call them and say, "Thanks!"

The people I would like to thank are:

1. _____
2. _____
3. _____
4. _____
5. _____

Your affirmation for gratitude

"I am grateful for everything in my life, and I attract new abundance each and every day."

Your daily must-do

Your negative "mind chatter" dump has really been helping you clear out the thoughts that don't help you on a daily basis. It's also been good practice for focusing on positivity and, by extension, gratitude. Creating space in your mind for positive thoughts to flow in easily leads you to having the space to thoughtfully start practicing your "attitude of gratitude."

Your review

1. What were my personal highlights during this energetic phase?
2. What challenges did I face and how did I handle them?

3. What exciting new insights did I discover about myself?
4. What was my greatest achievement in this phase?
5. What is my commitment for the next phase?

Remember

By the end of this book, you will discover what inspires you and who you want to be—and then you'll achieve it.

Your checklist

A. Answer the question at the start of the chapter.
B. Complete Task 1: Caring for yourself.
C. Complete Task 2: Learning to love yourself.
D. Complete Task 3: Self-talk.
E. Complete Task 4: Defining love.
F. Complete Task 5: Asking for forgiveness.
G. Complete Task 6: Visualization.
H. Complete Task 7: The Gratitude Game.
I. Complete Task 8: An attitude of gratitude.
J. Complete Task 9: Practicing gratitude.
K. Write out affirmations and verbalize daily.
L. Daily must-do: "mind chatter" dump.
M. Complete review.

CHECKING IN YET AGAIN!

Before we look at how you can maintain the new life that you have created, it is worth going over your roadblocks, the Manifestation Tool, affirmations, and visualizations. These tools should become part of your life, as you will periodically need to check in with yourself and make sure you're still on track. Living a life you'll love will take some work—for the rest of your life—and it's work worth doing.

Roadblock exercise

For the full Roadblock exercise, go back and take a look if you need to refresh. If you don't need to do the whole exercise again, just keep this equation in mind:

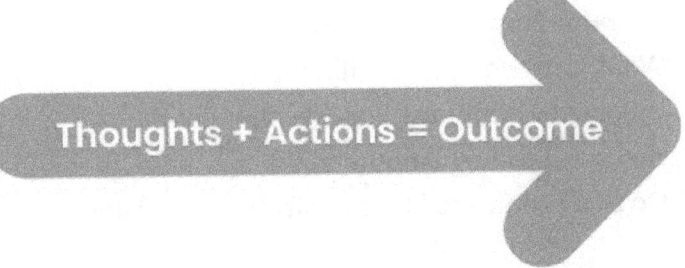

Thoughts + Actions = Outcome

The Manifestation Tool

Is the following equation still at the front of your mind?

My purpose + thoughts + vision + my words + feelings + actions + gratitude = goal.

Affirmations

Review the affirmations you have been working with. If you need to adjust them to reflect the changes you have already gone through, refer back to the Affirmations chapter.

Visualizations

If you haven't practiced visualizing the movie of your life recently, it's time to try it again. You may find that the movie has changed since the last time you "played" it—observe the changes but don't try to explain them to yourself and certainly don't make any judgments about what's changed.

The Five Dimensions of Wellness check

If you find that you're not flowing or connecting with yourself, do a five-dimension tune-up. Ask yourself:

1. How does my physical body feel?
2. What is my energy field like?
3. Where am I thinking negative thoughts?
4. How am I feeling emotionally?
5. Do I feel connected to my spiritual dimension?

You can put a new plan together to get yourself back in the flow using the tools you have already worked with in this book.

You should use the different tasks and tools as many times as you need—there's no right or wrong here. So that you don't push yourself or become out of balance, stop and ask yourself:

- What is it that I need right now?
- Where am I lacking?
- Where do I feel disconnected?
- Where do I feel not in the flow?

If you take just five minutes a day to answer these questions, you'll uncover the misalignment that is making you uncomfortable, and you'll be able to address the issue and make the right steps toward getting back in your flow.

PART IV
MAINTAINING BALANCE

THE BALANCED LIFE

A balanced life is a life that feels effortless despite the day-to-day activities, the traffic jams, the letdowns and missteps. Balance feels like everything in life is in alignment and achievable. Whenever we feel this balance in our lives, we recognize a sense of contentment and ease, and this is what we've strived for throughout the work we've done together.

At this stage of your personal journey, you will have identified clear goals for yourself and the strategies you need to employ to achieve them. You have unlocked any roadblocks in the way and uncovered a more balanced life and a more loving you. Learning and holding balance in your life is the final step in your transformation—building a structure and systems that support the new you so you can maintain your magnificence and shine your light daily—because there is no one else like you in the world.

To maintain all the positive changes in your life that you have worked hard to transform over the last few days, weeks, or months—however long it has taken you to work your way through this book—it's important to live a life that inspires you, and to create a glorious space for it to blossom inside yourself and within your surroundings. There is no "right" way to create and maintain balance. There is only your way and I urge you to take time to find what works for you. The point is to have a lifestyle that is balanced so that you provide the best possible "home" for your spirit. You have worked hard and now it's time to integrate all that hard work into your day-to-day living.

When you are in a state of balance and challenges come along, as they invariably do, you want to be able to face them in a responsive manner as opposed to a reactive manner. You will be able to see and deal with them from a place of equanimity and calm, not a place of fear and pain.

Finding a regimen of diet, exercise, work, and fun that is right for you will go a long way toward maintaining the balance that we all want to achieve. A life in balance is about finding a lifestyle that works for your unique body and sustaining it over the long term. There are many people in the world who will swear by a certain fad diet, a particular type of exercise, or a magic cure-all that has turned their life around, that it may have worked wonders for them, but that doesn't mean that it will work wonders for you. When something feels joyful and effortless, generally you'll find that you've achieved balance. This means, of course, that you don't discount treats from time to time, but they need to feed your balance and not tip into over-indulgence. That feeling of over-indulgence is a clear and obvious sign that you're out of balance. Recognize it—it's a great way to identify that you're in need of some adjustment.

Balance is also about giving and receiving. If you only ever give and you don't allow yourself to receive, your life is going to be out of balance. If you are all or nothing, your life is going to be out of balance. Most of us are very good at giving but struggle with receiving, and that comes down to not feeling worthy, or deserving, of love. This is a roadblock that many of us come face-to-face with throughout our lives. Tragically, I feel that it has almost become a universal hardship, one that is so unnecessary.

It's also important to remember that fear sneaking back in, like a dark cloud looming over you, is normal. It's just another way that your own self-doubt will be trying to upset that beautiful balance that you've created. So, pause and take a moment to breathe. There's no need to try and disconnect from it and pretend it doesn't exist. That will only allow the fear to grow unnecessarily. Rather, bring your awareness to the fear and acknowledge its existence. Say to yourself, "You know what? It's just a fear. Hi, how are you! I'm okay. I know you're around and I've had a great relationship with you, but I'm new now. I've got new tools." Just don't dismiss it because there could be a lesson here waiting to be learned.

Personally, I know that when I'm shining my light, my energy is clear and strong, and I am allowing the joy to flow through me, then it is the best version of me that is living life. I also know that when I'm not maintaining my life, it stops flowing and life becomes more difficult—it's just not as easy.

When I'm feeling unbalanced, it presents as fatigue in my life. I'll feel tired, stressed, and physically drained. The first thing I do is look at my level of self-care: how I have been sleeping lately, what my daily hydration is like, where's my diet at, have I been overbooking my diary. These things are all pretty straightforward and simple to remedy. I need to make the conscious effort to go to bed earlier, drink more water, ditch the unhealthy food, and push some of those unnecessary meetings to a less busy time in my schedule.

I'll also take a bit of a deeper dive into things and make more of an effort around some healthier choices in my life: a little less screen time, some time blocked out to just potter around the house, go for a walk, take a swim, read a book, or sit on the couch and watch a movie.

My approach to a feeling of imbalance is to literally write a list of things that are contributing to the imbalance and planning out how to alleviate the stress in my life. I find committing this to paper makes me see more clearly where the issues are and how to fix them. It also helps me to see that the issues aren't actually as big and scary as I first thought and that I am quite capable of making the necessary adjustments in my life.

To achieve greatness and magnificence requires your total commitment and dedication. It's essential to successfully achieving balance in your life by finding the best system for you to operate in. What works for me, your brother, or other people may not be right for you. Don't feel intimidated by the differences; embrace the uniqueness and strive toward finding your level. Life will feel balanced when you are relatively satisfied with all the important aspects of your life: physical, energetic, intellectual, emotional, and spiritual. No matter how busy you are, life feels in balance when you honor your values.

Your story

I have had the privilege to witness hundreds of people change their lives for the better by doing the work that has been outlined in this book. Literally, hundreds! These are people who have stopped and taken a long, investigative look at their lives and decided that they needed more. Just like you, they were ready to live lives that they truly loved.

One of the final steps toward implementing a daily routine is identifying and maintaining balance. It's important to remember that balance is different for everyone. What works for one person is not necessarily going to work for someone else. The final feeling of being in balance is the same, but how you get there will be different. If you're feeling depleted of energy, if you're sick all the time, if you feel stressed all the time, if you live in reaction all the time, clearly you are out of balance.

The questions you can ask yourself are:

- What do I need to do to bring my life back into balance?
- If I'm feeling stressed, what are the factors that are triggering me?
- What can I actually do about them, instead of playing victim to it?
- What can I do to change the situation?

Stop and ask yourself what you can do to bring your life back into balance. It's not enough to just do the work and sit back to wait for change to happen. You need to maintain the changes you have implemented, and it really isn't hard to do. The following tasks will help.

Task 1: Keeping on track

Here's a quick, straightforward way to get a handle on your important values and help you maintain your hard-earned transformation. I use this exercise as a quick check-in to keep me on track.

1. What is important to your life

    Make a list, not of what's nice but what must be in your life for you to be happy. It might be love, fascinating work, honesty, or friends. When you finish your list, go back over it and cut it in half. Now cut your list in half again. Repeat it until you have five or six words or phrases remaining. These are your critical values. Life will feel balanced when what you do revolves around, and includes, these values.

2. Passion

    What do you love to do? What activities so capture your attention and energy that you lose track of time while doing them? Make a list of these activities and divide your list into groups based on the level of passion you feel while involved in them. For example, it may be satisfying to organize your workspace and shred old files, but it may be joyous to sing in the choir. Look for common threads among the activities. Perhaps creativity is common to many, or adventure, or learning. When you strive to include your passions in your everyday, you'll have fewer days feeling overwhelmed and out of balance.

3. Strengths

    We each have unique strengths and talents. Your combination of special skills, interests, and inherent abilities make you unique. You have many competencies, but just a few unique strengths. When you use those few top strengths, your life will feel balanced. What are your unique strengths, skills, and talents?

4. Say no

    Many people find it hard to say no, so they end up taking on tasks that interfere with the important aspects of their lives and then they feel resentful and guilty. Learn to say no politely and firmly. Simply say, "I'm so sorry, I can't take that on just now and give it the attention and energy it deserves. Thank you for thinking of me." Then recommend someone else who might be qualified to do the task.

Task 2: Your energy levels

Review these areas of your life and decide what needs changing for you to feel the best you can feel. All of these things will affect your energy levels, which are important to maintain so all your efforts keep on working for you. A person who is happy and feels successful puts time aside for their health, for themselves, for learning and development, and also values their energy by choosing things that support them and give them a boost. Find as many things as you can that make you feel great.

- Foods you eat
- Alcohol intake
- Water you drink
- Exercise
- Sleep and relaxation activities
- Meditation, prayer, spiritual practice
- Reading, writing, creating
- Time spent doing non-work things like hobbies and playing. How much time do you spend accessing the child in you at play?
- Work, and how you feel about it
- Family: how do you feel about your family?
- Who do you need to forgive?
- Your home and how it is set up. Does it work for you?
- Do you have a sacred space to be?

Task 3: The life-balance checklist

Now, acknowledge the areas you have grown in. If there are still areas you would like to keep improving, use this list as a reflection guide and keep referring to it, re-evaluating each month after you have completed this book.

Put T (True) of F (False) next to these points:

- I spend time doing the things I love to do.
- I have nourishing relationships.
- I believe I can support myself financially, physically, emotionally, and spiritually.
- I feel happy with my appearance.
- I visit the dentist, optometrist, and doctor for regular check-ups.
- I have at least three holidays or breaks per year.
- I eat healthy foods.
- I leave work at work.
- I communicate my feelings honestly.
- I make time for physical exercise.
- I don't have any outstanding issues that need resolving.
- I have enough time.
- I treat myself each week to something I enjoy.
- I easily say no and cancel non-urgent appointments.
- I laugh with my friends each week.
- I surround myself with beautiful things.
- I feel calm and focused.
- I have high energy.
- I tell the people in my life that I love them daily.

Task 4: Your ideal week

To support your new life and values, it's important to create space to honor the new you. It has been a long journey over the course of this book discovering more aspects of who you are. Now get out your diary and block out space to honor the new you.

Fill out your ideal week and write in everything you need to maintain a powerful and strong relationship with yourself. For those who choose to work full-time, it's important to block out this time to maintain a vital you, even among the corporate jungle!

Here's an example, if you need it:

Monday

- Affirmations
- Journal writing
- Meditation
- Take home-made salad to work today
- Do a yoga class at lunchtime
- Write my Intention list of everything I would like to achieve for the next day

Tuesday

- Affirmation
- Journal writing
- Meditation
- Take home-made salad to work
- Work
- Write my Intention list of everything I would like to achieve for the next day
- After-work date with a friend who boosts my energy

Wednesday

- Affirmation
- Journal writing
- Meditation
- Work
- Write my Intention list of everything I would like to achieve for the next day
- Yoga class with a friend
- Watch a funny movie

Thursday

- Affirmations
- Journal writing
- Meditation
- Take healthy lunch to work
- Write my Intention list of everything I would like to achieve for the next day
- Finish work early and take the afternoon off
- Have a massage and facial

Friday

- Affirmations
- Journal writing
- Meditation
- Take a break at lunchtime and have lunch in the park while I refuel my being

Saturday

- Do a grocery shop and buy foods that support and nourish my being

- Block out an afternoon date on the couch with my favorite book
- Catch up with friends for dinner and a movie

Sunday
- Do a yoga class with friends followed by brunch
- Do an ocean swim and let my body be nourished by the salt water
- Have a siesta in the afternoon on the grass with my favorite podcast

In your notebook or journal, create your ideal week and include everything you need to nourish you and maintain vitality.

The brutal truth

If you've been doing all the steps in this book for six months and you are not seeing the results you want, you need to look at where you're potentially sabotaging yourself. Review your roadblocks. If you've come to this point and it's not working, always use the Roadblock exercise to see where you may be out of alignment. It could be that behind the scenes you're thinking negative thoughts. Be mindful that wherever you put your focus, that's going to be the greatest impact point.

If you truly are feeling that the results are not flowing, the Roadblock exercise will help you only in kindness and honesty. Approach it with compassion, not derision, to get the most effectiveness from the exercise. You've worked hard up until this point and there is no reason to undermine that work with harsh treatment of yourself for no reason.

Your affirmation for balance

"I honor myself and see my life as a powerful reflection of who I am."

Your daily must-do

"Mind chatter" dump! You know the drill.

Your review

1. What were my personal highlights during this balance phase?
2. What challenges did I face and how did I handle them?
3. What exciting new insights did I discover about myself?
4. What was my greatest achievement in this phase?
5. What is my commitment for the next phase?

Remember

By the end of this book, you will discover what inspires you and who you want to be—and then you'll achieve it.

Your checklist

A. Complete Task 1: Keeping on track.
B. Complete Task 2: Your energy levels.
C. Complete Task 3: The life-balance checklist.
D. Complete Task 4: Your ideal week.
E. Write out affirmation and verbalize daily.
F. Daily must-do: "mind chatter" dump.
G. Complete review.

LIVING IN FLOW

Now that you have arrived at the end of this book, it's safe to say that you have done a lot of work, made a lot of discoveries, and gone through some changes. That change is still happening, and it's all good.

You may have found some of the work confronting and difficult. You may even feel that you don't yet have a life you love and that's okay, because you are working toward it. It doesn't happen at the same pace for everyone. Before we leave each other, though, I wanted to give you a tip on how you can recognize when you are living a life you love, because there won't be any big banners in the sky or a special noise telling you that you have arrived at that life.

When we learn to flow in life, people are generally happier. It's impossible to tell you how the flow feels if you have not felt it. Once you have felt it, though—once you have lived it—you will know exactly what I'm talking about. This flow happens when we're living in the present moment and unattached to life's circumstances or how our prayers are to be answered. That is not to say that being in the flow means that we ignore our feelings when emotional events come into our lives; rather, we choose to ask a loving Universe (or whatever your sense of spirit responds to, be it Buddha, Jesus Christ or God, Source, etc.) for the highest and best results in every situation. The secret is realizing and viewing our Universe as all-loving and supportive, that opens doors within ourselves to receive the exact support we require in that moment. We release feelings of heaviness and ask The Universe to show us how we are supported. As we release harsh judgments on people and situations, we also release our "make it happen or else" approach. If we are not attached to the outcome, it allows us to receive the highest flow possible through spirit. Then things happen that we would have never imagined or ever thought possible.

When we notice patterns of synchronicity, we are clearly aligning with the natural state of flow that actually governs the cosmos. The best way to allow this to happen with ease is a combination of nurturing our physical, emotional, and spiritual habits on a daily basis. A daily practice of nutrition, rest, exercise, meditation, journaling, affirmations, and even tidying, cleaning up, and making the effort to practice utmost self-care can, in a matter of weeks, completely turn your life around into a state of greater flow.

You will notice that in flow, everything seems close to effortless. So-called "chance meetings" may bring about *déjà vu* and you might find that you are picking up on signs, symbols, patterns, and moments that would otherwise have seemed like strokes of unadulterated "good luck"; however, the fact is you are simply attracting what's meant for you in terms of your higher destiny.

When you have trained your body, mind, and spirit to access this state of natural flow (which is our birthright), you will find that you really do start to feel (as Lao Tzu and other spiritual philosophers have noted over the centuries) like "a leaf floating on water," living with calm and joy in a stress-free manner.

Surrendering to this process based on a foundation of daily, supportive habits, we acknowledge that we have actually raised our vibrational frequency and then we can start to make some serious progress in life goals, but with the sense that it's a glorious jigsaw puzzle into which the pieces are, quite literally, falling into place, seemingly all by themselves!

Our daily habits and increasing awareness of the power of good choices, and their ability to have an exponentially positive effect on our lives, create the framework within which magic can start to really happen.

As we make this vibrational frequency in every cell of our bodies move on a faster and higher level, the pace with which transformation occurs can at first be astounding. However, trust me when I say that you will become very accustomed to an increasingly fast pace of positive changes occurring once you start on that new trajectory.

If you are not willing to accept mediocrity in life and/or from yourself, you will see rapid transformation as you are rewarded with the fruits of transformation.

Let me give you some specific examples. You might find that, in a heightened state of flow, you start attracting people who seem to be actively out to help you! You might meet someone, say, at an airport who gives you a nice compliment on your shoes while standing in the queue and then you find that you strike up a bit of small talk together which leads to some mutual sharing of useful tips or contacts that help to take you a step further in a special project or concept you might be working on.

You might find that in a state of flow, you get a phone call from an unexpected source or an old friend who has something in mind for you which could be key to the next developmental phase in your work or personal life.

Being in flow for me is when I feel a general sense of ease within myself and in my day. My stress is at a minimum, I feel like the things I'm desiring to manifest are coming to me easily, that synchronicity is showing up in my day-to-day living. I feel like there are no rough edges to my life, that the calm, peace, and mindfulness that I have been consciously working for is present without effort or force.

Look around you right now and see if something is trying to "speak to you" through an image, a color, a pattern, or a word you see right in front of you. It's about becoming more and more attuned to the subtleties of your awareness and being willing to see things that are "hiding in plain sight." Once you start tuning in more, you'll find yourself feeling increasingly comfortable and more willing to trust that what you're feeling and seeing is real, because it is! You'll increasingly be finding yourself saying "magic happens" and "healing happens" as you notice the power of being in a state of flow.

We are what we attract. If we choose to emanate positivity, we can't help but attract that same positive energy. Try it and see how quickly things turn around for you in every aspect of your life.

You know when you are living in a state of flow when:

- Your day-to-day experiences seamlessly connect with less rushing around.
- You start experiencing better health and notice higher energy levels in your body.
- You start dealing with situations more effortlessly (even those which may have previously stressed you out in the past).

- You go with your gut instinct more often to make decisions.
- Your eyes shine and your skin starts to look hydrated, refreshed, and more radiant from within.
- You find yourself getting along with others much more easily.
- You get through your to-do lists with ease.
- Managing your schedule becomes a piece of cake as opposed to a nightmare.
- You start to see your dreams become reality.
- You carry a certain lightness of being which in turn sees you attracting like-minded people and experiences that add to the ease and joy of your life on a daily basis.

You know that it's time to take charge and align with a state of natural flow when:

- Living, in general, seems overwhelming.
- Your stress levels skyrocket.
- Your regular routine is annoying on every level.
- You feel like you can't trust your own decisions.
- You feel like discord and drama are bombarding you left, right, and center.
- Your energy levels seem depleted.
- You feel unable to stop worrying.
- Getting along with others seems harder and harder.
- You notice a lack of spontaneity and fun in life.
- You seem to attract misunderstandings, accidents, or negativity in general.

Being in the flow takes five steps:

1. Stop, observe, and inquire what's preventing the flow:
   - Am I thinking negative thoughts?
   - Am I feeling depleted in my energy?
   - Am I letting fear lead the way?
   - Am I listening to my inner critic instead of my intuition?

2. Check in with your true self for guidance.

3. Take action that you trust is being called for.

4. Having faith, excitement, and anticipation about the fabulous things on the horizon that your actions are leading you to.

5. Being grateful for the gifts that it brings and all the gifts you have in your life right now. Being in the flow is a relationship that you build and nurture every day to anchor yourself as opposed to living life in struggle.

Living in the flow opens you up to new opportunities but it does not happen automatically. You have just done a whole lot of work to make yourself ready for being in a state of flow and once you're in it, you need to maintain it. Sometimes you will fall out of the flow—but you can always step back in. And once you've lived in the flow, you'll never want to be out of it again.

A final word

On the days when you are lacking courage to live the life you love, don't judge yourself or despair. Remember that a wonderful life doesn't happen automatically—you will be working at this for the rest of your days. Remember, there is no more important work for you to do than creating a life you love.

It's been my pleasure to have journeyed alongside you. I have cheered you on with enthusiasm, love, and the belief that you have more inside of you than you have allowed yourself to imagine. You have done all the hard work and positioned yourself for a life lived well. Be your beautiful brave self. You've earned it!

Hello Coach

🌐 https://hello-coach.com

✉ victoria@hello-coach.com

in https://au.linkedin.com/company/hellocoachworld

📷 https://www.instagram.com/hellocoachworld

www.ingramcontent.com/pod-product-compliance
Lightning Source LLC
Chambersburg PA
CBHW050304010526
44107CB00055B/2100